Cambridge Elements ≡

Elements in Religion and Monotheism
edited by
Paul K. Moser
Loyola University Chicago
Chad Meister
*Affiliate Scholar, Ansari Institute for Global Engagement with Religion,
University of Notre Dame*

OPEN THEISM

Alan R. Rhoda
Christian Theological Seminary

CAMBRIDGE
UNIVERSITY PRESS

CAMBRIDGE
UNIVERSITY PRESS

Shaftesbury Road, Cambridge CB2 8EA, United Kingdom

One Liberty Plaza, 20th Floor, New York, NY 10006, USA

477 Williamstown Road, Port Melbourne, VIC 3207, Australia

314–321, 3rd Floor, Plot 3, Splendor Forum, Jasola District Centre, New Delhi – 110025, India

103 Penang Road, #05–06/07, Visioncrest Commercial, Singapore 238467

Cambridge University Press is part of Cambridge University Press & Assessment, a department of the University of Cambridge.

We share the University's mission to contribute to society through the pursuit of education, learning and research at the highest international levels of excellence.

www.cambridge.org
Information on this title: www.cambridge.org/9781009494816

DOI: 10.1017/9781009349390

First published 2024

A catalogue record for this publication is available from the British Library.

ISBN 978-1-009-49481-6 Hardback
ISBN 978-1-009-34938-3 Paperback
ISSN 2631-3014 (online)
ISSN 2631-3006 (print)

Open Theism

Elements in Religion and Monotheism

DOI: 10.1017/9781009349390
First published online: February 2024

Alan R. Rhoda
Christian Theological Seminary
Author for correspondence: Alan R. Rhoda, arhoda@cts.edu

Abstract: This Element presents open theism as a monotheist model of God according to which the future is objectively open-ended, not just from the finite perspective of creation, but from God's perspective as well. This Element has three main sections. The first carefully defines open theism, distinguishes its major variants, compares it to other monotheistic models, and summarizes its history. The second develops biblical and philosophical arguments for open theism against its main rivals, emphasizing a novel philosophical argument that a causally open future must also be ontically, alethically, epistemically, and providentially open as well. The third responds to common objections against open theism related to perfect being theology, the ethics of risk-taking, biblical prophecy, and theological tradition.

This Element also has a video abstract: www.Cambridge.org/ERM_Rhoda

Keywords: open theism, open future, foreknowledge, future contingents, fatalism

ISBNs: 9781009494816 (HB), 9781009349383 (PB), 9781009349390 (OC)
ISSNs: 2631-3014 (online), 2631-3006 (print)

Contents

1 Introduction

"Open theism," as it is now standardly called, is a monotheistic model of God and of divine providence that goes back at least 1,600 years. It remained a small minority position until the publication of Pinnock *et al.* (1994), which generated a firestorm of controversy, particularly in the North American evangelical community (Schmid, 2021: 1–9). That book and the controversy it generated brought open theism to the wide attention of philosophical and theological scholars. Within the contexts of philosophy of religion and analytic theology, open theism is now recognized as a major player alongside other competing models of God and divine providence, such as theistic determinism, Molinism, and process theism.

Roughly stated, open theism holds that the future of creation is open-ended, not just from a creaturely perspective, but from God's as well. Open theism thus challenges the widespread theological idea that God has "exhaustive definite foreknowledge" (EDF).[1] Exhaustive definite foreknowledge has two components. First, EDF says God has exhaustive and infallible knowledge of the future. This is about the *nature* of God's knowledge, namely, its scope (exhaustive) and quality (infallible). Second, EDF says that the future as God knows it is exhaustively definite. In other words, there is a unique *future* – a unique and complete linear extension of the actual past and present – that shall come to pass. This is about the *content* of God's knowledge, namely, that the future God foreknows includes or specifies a fully determinate future timeline, the "unique actual future" (UAF). Open theists reject EDF by denying one or both of its components, with some open theists saying there is no UAF but rather a future of branching possibilities and others saying there is a UAF, but that God does not and perhaps cannot know it. In either case, open theists hold that the future is open-ended from God's perspective and by God's design to facilitate two-way interrelationality between God and free creatures.

As this is a short Element about open theism and because I have much to say on the topic, I have to be selective in my focus. Because I am a philosopher by training and not a biblical scholar or systematic theologian, I focus on open theism as a philosophical model of divine providence. My primary goal is to provide a philosophically rigorous articulation and defense of open theism. Due to space constraints, I have skipped over some issues (e.g., open theism's practical relevance for religious life) and treated other issues (e.g., open theism's relevance for the problem of evil) more briefly than I would have liked.

In Section 2 I explain what open theism is. I define its core tenets, distinguish its most important variants, contrast it with other models of divine providence,

---

[1] The EDF phrase was coined by Boyd (1997: 49–50, 304).

and finally summarize the history of open theism in relation to the great monotheistic traditions of Judaism, Christianity, and Islam.

In Section 3 I develop a systematic case *for* open theism over against its main competitors. I start by surveying six categories of biblical passages that suggest God faces a providentially and/or epistemically open future. I then present a philosophical case for future contingency and creaturely libertarian freedom (*pace* theistic determinism), culminating in reflections on the problem of moral evil. Finally, I target models that attempt to combine EDF and future contingency (Molinism, simple foreknowledge, etc.) by arguing that the mere existence of a UAF is incompatible with future contingency. This implies not only the falsity of EDF (given future contingency) but also the untenability of UAF-affirming versions of open theism.

In Section 4 I discuss and rebut four common objections to open theism. First, that it conflicts with perfect being theology and thus "diminishes" God (Ware, 2000). Second, that open theism is too risky for, despite the best intentions, an open theistic God could "bodge" things up quite badly (Mawson, 2019). Third, that open theism cannot make adequate sense of scriptural prophecy. And fourth, that it is too radical a departure from the mainstream theological tradition. In rebuttal I argue that open theism is compatible with perfect being theology and that arguments to the contrary are unconvincing, that reflections on the ethics of risk-taking and God's resources for managing creation effectively defuse the charge that open theism is too risky, that open theism can plausibly accommodate scriptural prophecy, and that open theism should qualify as an admissible theological opinion even on a robustly normative view of the early Christian theological tradition.[2]

2 Open Theism Explained

Open theism is (a) a monotheistic version of *theism*. What makes open theism *open* is that it affirms both (b) the open-endedness of God's creation and (c) the intrinsic openness or responsiveness of God to that creation. This, however, is only a rough characterization. We need to flesh out (a)–(c) to make it precise enough for assessment and comparison with competing models. To that end, I begin by articulating open theism's hard core, which I call *mere* open theism (cf. Rhoda, 2008). Following that, I distinguish several important variants of open theism, compare open theism with other models of divine providence, and finally give a brief historical overview.

---

[2] I thank Elijah Hess, Ryan Mullins, John Sanders, Patrick Todd, and two referees for generous comments.

2.1 Mere Open Theism

Proponents and critics of open theism frequently generalize about what open theism is or entails. Very often these generalizations lack precision and accuracy. For example, while the claim that the God of open theism "lacks comprehensive foreknowledge" (Anderson, 2019: 121) aptly describes what *some* open theists believe, many open theists would emphatically deny it, holding instead that God does have comprehensive foreknowledge. They would just add that the *content* of God's foreknowledge is not what EDF proponents suppose. The issue, they say, is not *whether* God has comprehensive foreknowledge but *what it means* to have comprehensive foreknowledge. Similarly, many discussions about God's knowledge of "the future" assume this refers to a unique actual future (UAF), which begs the question against open theists who deny there is any such thing. It's not that they deny that anything can properly be *called* "the future." Rather, they take "the future" to refer to a branching array of possibilities (Rhoda *et al.*, 2006). To have a productive discussion of open theism – its variants, merits, and challenges – without different sides talking past each other, it is necessary that we define the essentials of open theism before diving into polemical matters.

For starters, open theism is a version of *theism*. More exactly, it's a version of what I call *minimal monotheism*:

(1)   Minimal monotheism $=_{def}$. There is exactly one God who is personal, who exists necessarily, and to whom all other beings ultimately owe their existence. God is essentially maximally excellent with respect to goodness, power, and knowledge. God freely created the world ex nihilo and can unilaterally intervene in it.

This is a standard monotheistic account such as would be endorsed by nearly all Jews, Christians, and Muslims who have thought carefully about God. Most such theists would want to say quite a bit *more* about God, but nearly all would agree with this *as far as it goes*. By "exists necessarily" I mean merely that God never began to exist and cannot cease existing. By "essentially maximally excellent" I mean that God essentially excels in goodness, power, and knowledge to the greatest metaphysically possible degree given only the need for internal consistency (Nagasawa, 2017). In the final sentence I specify creation ex nihilo and God's unilateral power to intervene to *exclude* process theism, which standardly holds that God and the world process always coexist in a metaphysically necessary symbiosis, with God only able to influence the world process "persuasively" and never "coercively" or unilaterally (Cobb & Griffin, 1976). In contrast, the founders of the modern open theism movement have been clear that, while open theism sits somewhere between the classical theism of high medieval orthodoxy and process theism, they mean to stay squarely on the classical side with respect to God's power over creation.[3] As I put it elsewhere, "open theists have generally seen their view as a relatively *conservative* modification or correction of the classical tradition ... for the purpose of resolving what they see as otherwise irresolvable ... tensions within that tradition" (Rhoda, 2008: 226).

The next five tenets are what put the "open" in open theism. Three of them belong to the hard core of mere open theism. The other two would be endorsed by *most* open theists, but I leave them out of the core to accommodate versions of open theism that might not affirm them.

These tenets define five types of openness using the concept of *a* "future" (note the indefinite article), that is, a complete, linear extension of the actual past and present. An *abstract* future is a logically consistent *proposition* fully describing a complete, linear way events could unfold from the present on.[4] A *concrete* future is a complete, linear sequence of post-present *events*. Normally I have abstract futures in mind. When I need to speak of concrete futures, I describe them as such. Further, when I speak of *the* future (note the definite article) I mean the collection of futures compatible with all future-relevant facts, where a "future-relevant fact" is anything actual that bears upon what happens subsequently. This conception of the future is *neutral* with respect to whether there is a UAF. If only one future is compatible with all future-relevant facts, then there is a UAF; otherwise, there is no UAF. Whether there is a UAF, therefore, depends on what future-relevant facts there are. When I do need to speak of the future in a way that implies a UAF, such as when describing views that contrast with open theism, I make that clear by speaking of "the UAF" or "the unique actual future" rather than simply "the future." Finally, when I speak of the future as "open" or "settled" in some particular way (e.g., causally), I mean to *restrict* the scope of future-relevant facts to those of the specified type (e.g., the causal ones).

---

[3] I take the *founders* of modern open theism to include the five coauthors of Pinnock *et al.* (1994) – Clark Pinnock, Richard Rice, John Sanders, William Hasker, and David Basinger – and Greg Boyd. Influential works on open theism by these authors include Boyd (2001), Pinnock (2001), Sanders (1998; 2007), Rice (1985), and Hasker (1989). For their views on divine power over against process theism, see Pinnock *et al.* (1994: 138–141), Cobb and Pinnock (2000), Basinger (1988), and Boyd (2001: 31).

[4] When I speak of *the* present, I'm deliberately sidelining Einsteinian relativity, for the issues of open theism have to do with *God's* perspective on time, not that of human physicists. Einstein posited the relativity of the *empirical* present because the finite speed of light prevents *us* from experimentally identifying an objective *metaphysical* present. But an essentially maximal knower like God doesn't face such limitations. If God exists temporally and thus has a temporal perspective, then I see no reason not to equate God's present with the objective metaphysical present. For further reasons why Einsteinian relativity does not preclude an objective metaphysical present, see Craig and Smith (2008).

In the first place, then, *all* open theists hold that the future is *causally open*:

(2)   Causal openness of the future. The future is *causally open* as of time t $=_{def}$. There are multiple causally possible futures relative to t.

By "causally possible futures" I mean those compatible with all explanatorily prior *causal* constraints on what can happen after t. Such constraints include the conditions at t, stable natural laws, and any supernatural causal factors bearing upon the future. My notion of causal openness is intended to include *both* primary (supernatural) and secondary (natural) causation. To say that there are *multiple* causally possible futures is to say that causal determinism is false at both the natural and supernatural levels and that causal indeterminism is true at both levels. It is also to say that there are *future contingents*, that is, causally possible events that occur on some causally possible futures but not others. For example, if the occurrence of a sea battle tomorrow is, as of now, a future contingent, then there are causally possible futures in which a sea battle occurs tomorrow and causally possible futures in which no sea battle occurs tomorrow. Both outcomes are causally possible, neither is causally necessary, and the future is thus causally open with respect to whether a sea battle occurs tomorrow. If, however, at 11:59 p.m. tonight circumstances change such that a sea battle tomorrow is now causally inevitable (e.g., the admiral has given the order to attack in such a way that it cannot be rescinded in time), then it would no longer be a future contingent. The set of causally possible futures relative to *that* time would not include any without a sea battle tomorrow.

Now, while (nearly) all open theists believe the most important source of causal openness is creaturely *libertarian* free will, I do not consider libertarian free will to be part of the hard core of *mere* open theism. Libertarianism entails causal openness because it is *incompatibilist*. That is, libertarianism holds that the sort of free will necessary for grounding moral responsibility is incompatible with causal determinism and therefore requires causal indeterminism, which entails causal openness.[5] But I see no reason to think a minimal monotheist couldn't be an open theist for reasons concerning causal indeterminism in general. In short, even if one thinks creaturely free will (of the sort necessary for grounding moral responsibility) is *compatible* with causal determinism, one could still be an open theist provided one thinks some events (e.g., quantum events) are *not* causally determined and satisfies the other requirements of mere open theism.

---

[5] Some self-professed libertarians, for example, McCann (2005), affirm causal openness at the secondary causal level but not at the primary causal level. Against this I simply *stipulate* that I take libertarianism to imply causal openness at both levels. One cannot, as I use the term, be both a libertarian and a theistic determinist.

In the second place, *most*, but not necessarily all, open theists hold that the future is *ontically open*.

(3)   Ontic openness of the future. The future is *ontically open* as of time $t =_{def}$. No unique concrete future relative to t *exists*.

The italicized "exists" in (3) is to be understood in the *unrestricted quantifier* sense. (3) says that, if we consider the full inventory of reality from an absolute or "God's eye" perspective, it includes all present events, and perhaps all past events, but does *not* include a unique and complete sequence of future events. Consequently, the ontic openness of the future entails that the eternalist or "block universe" view on which a unique and complete sequence of past, present, and future events tenselessly *exists*, is false. Most open theists hold to a *presentist* ontology of time according to which only present things exist, some hold to a *growing block* model according to which only past and present things exist, and an open theist could, in principle, hold to a *branching block* model according to which past and present events and *all causally possible concrete futures* exist, but no *unique* concrete future exists (McCall, 1994).

In the third place, *most*, but not all, open theists hold that the future is *alethically open*.

(4)   Alethic openness of the future. The future is *alethically open* as of time $t =_{def}$. No future relative to t is such that it is *true* that it is or shall be the unique actual future relative to t.

In other words, there is no such thing as a complete, true, linear "story of the future." The story of the actual past and present is finished and "published," so to speak, but the story of the future is unfinished. Some aspects of that story – the causally determined parts – can be inferred from what has already been written, but the future contingent parts are yet to be decided.

In the fourth place, *all* open theists hold that the future is *epistemically open*, not just for us, but even for a maximal knower like God.

(5)   Epistemic openness of the future. The future is *epistemically open* as of time $t =_{def}$. No future relative to t is *infallibly* known by God (or anyone else) to be or to be going to be the unique actual future relative to t.

This aspect of open theism has generated much controversy. I save defense of it for Sections 3 and 4. For now, it suffices to note that *if* (4) is true, then (5) is true as well because knowledge presupposes truth. This justification for (5), however, is not available to open theists who deny (4). Obviously, if (5) is true, then EDF is false for, as far as God knows, there remain *multiple* futures that could in due course become actual.

In the fifth place, *all* open theists hold that the future is *providentially open*. The future is causally open and epistemically open (and perhaps also ontically and alethically open) because *God wants it that way*.

(6) Providential openness of the future. The future is *providentially open* as of time $t =_{def}$. No single future relative to t has been selected by God (or anyone else) to be the unique actual future relative to t.

In other words, when choosing to create, God didn't actualize a *token* possible world with a complete, determinate history.[6] Rather, God set up a certain *type* of world by establishing its initial conditions, its causal constraints, and God's interaction policies with creation, but deliberately left *some* details of world history unspecified, *delegating* those details to creatures.

Of the five types of openness discussed, (2), (3), and (4) concern the openness *of the future*, whereas (5) and (6) concern the openness *of God* to creation. In terms of both knowledge (5) and will (6), God approaches the future as a somewhat open-ended project and looks to creation to fill in the remaining details. I only include (2), (5), and (6) – causal, epistemic, and providential openness – as parts of *mere* open theism, however, because some versions of open theism explicitly reject (4) (alethic openness) and others theoretically could reject (3) (ontic openness).

To finish articulating *mere* open theism, we need to reconcile an apparent conflict between (1) and (5). Statement (1), recall, says God is essentially maximally excellent with respect to *knowledge*. This creates a strong presumption that if something is knowable, then God knows it, and knows it as well as it can be known. So, for the future to be epistemically open for God, there must be a principled reason why EDF – infallible knowledge of a unique actual future – is not available to God. But given that God is also essentially maximally excellent with respect to *power* and creates the world ex nihilo, the open theist is committed to the idea that God *could have had* EDF simply by creating a causally determined world. In such a case, knowing the initial conditions and

---

[6] Following Plantinga (1974) and Lewis (1986a), it is often assumed that "possible worlds," or complete ways things could be, must include a complete, determinate history because they are *tenseless* entities that either determinately include or exclude every possible state of affairs, past, present, and future. But, as Seymour (2015) has shown, the notion of a "time" defined by Crisp (2007) qualifies as a *tensed* possible world because it determinately includes or excludes every possible state of affairs. Crispian times are, in essence, complete ways things could be *at a time*. One can therefore take the "actual world" to be the current total way things are *now* rather than the total way things (tenselessly) *are* throughout all of history. In so doing one replaces a *static* conception of the actual world with a *dynamic* one – which possible world is *the* actual world continually changes as the total way things are *now* changes.

the causal laws he set in place, God could have infallibly inferred the entire history of creation. So, the reason why God doesn't have EDF must lie in the fact that he has chosen to create a causally open world. This brings us to the final tenet of mere open theism:

(7)   Causal openness entails epistemic openness. More specifically, it is impossible that the future be epistemically *settled* in any respect in which it remains causally open.

By "settled" here I simply mean the complement of "open." For each type of openness defined in in (2)–(6), if the future is *not* causally, ontically, ..., etc. *open*, then it is causally, ontically, ..., etc. *settled*.[7]

To wrap up this section, let's revisit (1) and consider whether (2) causal, (5) epistemic, and (6) providential openness along with (7) imply anything about the *sort* of monotheism open theists are committed to. For starters, they imply that the strict "classical theism" of high medieval orthodoxy is false. Classical theists standardly hold that God is not only minimally monotheistic, but also *absolutely simple, absolutely immutable, absolutely impassible, and timelessly eternal*. I don't have space to unpack these concepts.[8] Suffice to say, open theists must reject all of these and replace them with something less absolute. The God of open theism cannot be timelessly eternal or absolutely immutable because the content of God's knowledge of creation *updates over time* as future contingencies are progressively resolved.[9] God is, however, immutable with respect to his essential perfections and eternal in the sense that God's existence has no beginning and no end. Nor can the God of open theism be absolutely impassible because, as (5) and (6) imply, God deliberately remains open to being affected by creation with respect to the content of his knowledge, which informs how God responds. God does, however, remain impassible with respect to his essential nature.[10] Finally, the God of open theism cannot be absolutely simple precisely because he is neither absolutely immutable nor absolutely impassible. Because the content of God's knowledge intrinsically changes over time, it follows that God has accidental intrinsic properties,

---

[7] I say "settled" rather than "closed" because the latter has negative connotations that are best avoided. What EDF proponent wants to say that the future is epistemically *closed* for God? That sounds more like a description of future ignorance than EDF.

[8] See Mullins (2016) for an in-depth explication of classical theism.

[9] Sanders (2007: 15) calls this aspect of open theism "dynamic omniscience."

[10] Creel (1986) distinguishes between impassibility in nature, will, knowledge, and feeling. Open theists can affirm impassibility with respect to God's nature and *antecedent* will (what God sovereignly decrees, including his contingency plans), but not impassibility with respect to God's knowledge or *consequent* will (how God responds to creaturely developments). Most open theists would also say God is passible in feeling and has appropriate emotional responses to creaturely events (cf. Mullins, 2020).

and so isn't *absolutely* simple. Instead, God is *mereologically* simple in virtue of having no proper or separable parts. God is an indissoluble unity.

Summing up, mere open theism is the conjunction of (1) minimal monotheism; the (2) causal, (5) epistemic, and (6) providential openness of the future; and (7) the incompatibility of causal openness with an epistemically settled future. Collectively, (2) and (5)–(7) flesh out the minimal monotheism of (1) by implying that God is, in some respects, both passible and mutable in virtue of being responsive to creation. I now consider several variants of mere open theism, which I henceforth simply call "open theism," thus dropping the "mere."

2.2 Major Variants of Open Theism

Given how I have defined open theism, there are as many ways of being an open theist as there are ways of adding to or further specifying the conjunction of (1), (2), (5), (6), and (7). In this section I distinguish several variants of open theism and give my reasons for preferring the variant that will serve as the focus of discussion moving forward.

In the first place, regarding the scope of God's knowledge, there are two main variants, each of which subdivides. The first main variant affirms God's *unqualified omniscience*. On this view God knows *everything* there is to know and knows it completely. That is, God infallibly knows *all* truths and is fully and immediately acquainted with *all* of reality. God's knowledge of the future is open-ended precisely because the future *is* open-ended. The future is thus both alethically and ontically open in addition to being causally, epistemically, and providentially open. Because it is alethically open, there is no *abstract* UAF. Because it is ontically open, there is no *concrete* UAF. Hence, there is no UAF period. Following Todd (2014), I'll call this *open future* open theism (OFOT) because it holds that the future is open in *all five* senses distinguished earlier. This is the more popular of the two main variants.[11]

Open future open theism subdivides between those who affirm bivalence for propositions about future contingents and those who deny bivalence. I'll call these subgroups *bivalentist* and *non-bivalentist*, respectively. Bivalentist open futurists believe *will* and *will not* propositions about future contingents are logical contraries, not true contradictories. Accordingly, both types of propositions are *false* so long as the events they concern remain causally contingent. What's true instead is a *might-and-might-not* proposition.[12] So, for example, if it is a future contingent whether a sea battle occurs tomorrow, then <There will

---

[11] Proponents of OFOT include Boyd (2010), Hasker (2021), Hess (2015), Rhoda (2008), Todd (2014), and Tuggy (2007).

[12] *Might* is used here *nonepistemically* to connote causal possibility.

be a sea battle tomorrow> and <There will not be a sea battle tomorrow> are both false, but <There might-and-might-not be a sea battle tomorrow> is true. In contrast, non-bivalentist open futurists hold that *will* and *will not* propositions about future contingents are logical contradictories and that they are *neither true nor false* because reality remains indeterminate in that respect.[13]

The second main variant of open theism affirms *qualified omniscience*. Proponents of this view say that, while God is an essentially maximally excellent knower, this does not mean God must know all truths or be fully acquainted with all of reality. Following Todd (2014), I'll call this *limited foreknowledge* open theism (LFOT). According to LFOT, the future is alethically settled, and possibly also ontically settled. Hence, there *is* a UAF – at least an abstract one and possibly also a concrete one – but God either does not or cannot know it.

Those who think God *cannot know* the UAF believe *will* and *will not* propositions about future contingents are *unknowable*.[14] Because these truths are unknowable, proponents of this view deny that God's *not* knowing them undermines his status as an essentially maximally excellent knower. Omniscience, on this view, is understood as knowing all *knowable* truths, rather than knowing all truths *simpliciter*.[15] Let's call this *nonvolitional* LFOT.

Those who think God *can but does not know* the UAF believe that *will* and *will not* propositions about future contingents are knowable by God but are not actually known because God doesn't *want* to know them. Because God *can* know all truths, proponents of this view deny that God's *not* knowing some of them undermines his status as an essentially maximally excellent knower. Omniscience, on this view, is understood as the *ability* to know all truths, rather than the state or condition of knowing all truths.[16] Let's call this *volitional* LFOT.

Another important distinction, one that cuts across the OFOT/LFOT divide, concerns how God exercises providence. Some open theists – most explicitly Boyd (2003) – hold that God does *exhaustive contingency planning* (ECP). On this view, which Boyd calls "neo-Molinism,"[17] God's creative decree is analogous to that of an infinitely intelligent chess master who, at the outset of the game before any moves have occurred, considers *all* causally possible ways the game could unfold and *predecides* his responses to every possible creaturely

---

[13] Boyd, Hess, Rhoda, and Todd are bivalentists. Tuggy and Hasker are non-bivalentists.

[14] In the context of what's knowable or unknowable by God, *infallible* knowledge is in view. Whether creatures can *fallibly* know the outcomes of some future contingencies is a separate question, one I do not here address, but see Rhoda (2017) for discussion.

[15] Swinburne (2016: 196), Hasker (1989: 187), van Inwagen (2008). Hasker (2021) has since changed his position.

[16] Willard (1998: 244–253) is the only contemporary open theist I know of who takes this line. Ramsay (1748) also defended it.

[17] See Hess (2015) for discussion.

"move."[18] Other open theists – most notably Sanders – hold that God does only *partial contingent planning* (PCP). On this view God does *not* predecide all his responses but engages in some degree of *ad hoc decision-making*. Arguably, PCP more closely reflects biblical passages that depict God as changing his mind and maintains an anthropomorphically more natural sense of God's responsiveness to creation (Sanders 2007: 229–246).

When combined, the preceding distinctions yield eight different "flavors" of open theism. I now give my reasons for preferring one of those over the others.

In the first place, I think OFOT is hands-down the way to go. Limited foreknowledge open theism suffers from three main weaknesses. First, by conceding that there are truths God does not know, LFOT plays into the hands of critics who charge that open theism makes God less than maximally excellent with respect to knowledge.[19] From the perspective of OFOT, this is an unforced dialectical error. Why concede the rhetorical high ground of perfect being theology to your opponents? In contrast to LFOT, OFOT holds that God infallibly knows *all* truths.[20] Open future open theism is thus immune to the charge that it diminishes God's omniscience. The debate then becomes not whether God *is* omniscient, but whether the *content* of God's omniscience specifies a UAF. This creates a better dialectical situation for open theists, who can argue that the future is open-ended from God's perspective precisely because the future *is* objectively open-ended. In other words, epistemic openness is a consequence of God's epistemic perfection.

Second, LFOT is poorly motivated in comparison with OFOT. By admitting that a UAF exists, LFOT raises the obvious question: why doesn't God know it? Prima facie we expect information to be accessible to a maximally excellent knower if the information exists. By denying that such information exists, OFOT has a straightforward answer to the question. Nonvolitional LFOT does not. Indeed, any reason one might give for thinking a maximally excellent knower like God *cannot* know the UAF is at least as good a reason for thinking there is no UAF.[21] Here volitional LFOT has an advantage over nonvolitional LFOT: the former can reply that God doesn't know the UAF because God doesn't *want* to. But this raises other awkward questions, such as how God can *selectively bracket* information that, as volitional LFOT admits, is there to be known any time God wants to access it. Does God start out knowing all truths and then self-induce partial amnesia so he no longer knows truths about the UAF he once knew? If so, then God would also have

---

[18] See Rhoda (2009) for critical discussion of the chess master analogy and other open theist analogies.

[19] I examine this objection in Section 4.1.

[20] More exactly, God infallibly knows of every true proposition that it is true (Swinburne, 2016: 177).

[21] Todd (2014) recommends LFOT proponents say God cannot know the UAF because there is *not enough evidence*. But the very conditions (namely, future contingency) that might be thought to create a lack of evidence sufficient for infallible knowledge of a UAF also undermine the idea that there is a UAF in the first place (Todd, 2021: 16–19).

to forget he forgot that information, lest he recover it by knowing what he forgot. But if God no longer knows the truths are there to be known, then in what sense *can* he still know them? And if God does *not* start out knowing all truths, then how does God still qualify as an *essentially* maximally excellent knower?

Third, LFOT fails to secure future contingency against the threat of fatalism. In Section 3.2 I show that there is a demonstrably valid argument for fatalism that allows only two antifatalist responses: open futurism and preventable futurism. By denying that there is a UAF, OFOT can give a consistently open futurist response to every possible fatalistic argument. Limited foreknowledge open theism, in contrast, gives an open futurist response to causal, epistemic, and providential arguments for fatalism, but a preventable futurist response to alethic (and possibly also ontic) arguments for fatalism. I argue further, however, that preventable futurism is only a *superficially* adequate response to fatalism. At a deeper level it is ontologically incoherent because the mere existence of a UAF is incompatible with future contingency. If my argument succeeds, then LFOT is implicitly inconsistent and thus false. Open future open theism has no such vulnerability.

Having argued that OFOT is to be preferred over LFOT, I now argue, in the second place, that exhaustive contingency planning (ECP) is better than partial contingency planning (PCP), at least when it comes to morally significant contingencies. Like an infinitely intelligent chess master who carefully thinks things through ahead of time, ECP helps God better manage the *risks* inherent in creating an open-ended world of morally free creatures. By choosing to create such a world, God risks that creatures will misuse their freedom to bring about moral evil or act in ways that, while not wrong per se, might inadvertently frustrate God's plans. Exhaustive contingency planning means that, prior to deciding to actualize any kind of world, God considers *every possible* creaturely situation that could arise and assesses how best to respond *in every case*. In so doing, God minimizes the risk that his plans for creation will fail and maximizes the chances that those plans will succeed without unnecessary collateral damage along the way. In contrast, God's doing only PCP is analogous to a chess AI that only looks *n* number of moves ahead and/or doesn't carefully evaluate every possible position. The danger is that some possibility beyond the *n*-move horizon and/or some nonevaluated possibility might be a "game changer." Likewise, God's doing only PCP would mean either *not considering* some creaturely possibilities from the outset or *not bothering* to assess how best to respond in some cases. The former raises a worry about God's knowledge and power. Is there any reason to think considering all creaturely possibilities is *difficult* for God? No. Being an essentially maximally excellent knower plausibly entails that God cannot *not* consider all possibilities. The latter raises a worry about God's goodness. Why wouldn't God bother to assess his response options in all cases? Is it because God doesn't really *care* how his choices might impact creatures for good or ill? That doesn't sound like maximally excellent goodness. But perhaps some contingencies are morally innocuous and have no material bearing on the success or failure of God's plans (e.g., how some quantum indeterminacy resolves in a lifeless galaxy far away). Because such trivial contingencies carry no serious risks, if there's moral room for PCP, that's most plausibly where it lies. But if there's no compelling reason for God to do ECP regarding trivial contingencies, then there's also no compelling reason for God *not* to do ECP in such cases. In sum, while ECP is not morally necessary across the board, it never hurts, whereas PCP is potentially disastrous if God fails to prepare for contingencies that are *not* trivial. To keep matters simple, I presuppose ECP moving forward.

Finally, with respect to OFOT, I think bivalentism is better than non-bivalentism. This issue doesn't matter for my purposes in this Element, but I have three reasons for preferring bivalentism. First, it doesn't require any adjustments to standard logic, whereas non-bivalentism requires giving up the law of excluded middle (LEM) in its truth-functional form.[22] Second, even if there are good reasons for denying bivalence in contexts involving objective vagueness (Smith, 2008), it is controversial whether there is objective vagueness, and even if there is, it has nothing to do with future contingency per se (Todd, 2021: 78–79). Finally, non-bivalentism for future contingencies typically rests on a principle that Todd calls *will excluded middle* (WEM).[23] He convincingly shows, however, that WEM is false as a *semantic* principle. If WEM is true, it is true for metaphysical reasons (like the future's being causally or ontically settled), not semantic ones (Todd, 2021: ch. 3). Because these metaphysical reasons are theses OFOT *denies*, given that OFOT is decisively better than LFOT, non-bivalentism for future contingencies remains poorly motivated.

I conclude that the best version of open theism is a bivalentist version of OFOT that affirms ECP. On this version, the future is open in *all five* senses discussed earlier (causal, ontic, alethic, epistemic, and providential), God has exhaustive knowledge of the open-ended future, and there is no UAF. God perfectly knows the future as open-ended because, and to the precise extent that, it is open-ended. Moreover, God has contingency plans in place for every possible creaturely situation, so there is no possibility of God's being caught flat-footed by unforeseen creaturely developments. Hereafter, when I speak of open theism, this is the version I have in mind unless specified otherwise. With that, I now compare open theism with other common models of divine providence.

---

[22] LEM says that, for all propositions *p*, either *p* or ~*p*. Truth-functionally understood, LEM is true only if one of its disjuncts is true. If neither is true, LEM fails.

[23] WEM says that, for all propositions *p*, either F*p* or F~*p*. Due to the position of the negation, however, this is not a proper instance of LEM unless F~*p* (i.e., it will be the case that not-*p*) is semantically equivalent to ~F*p* (i.e., it is not the case that it will be the case that *p*).

2.3 Open Theism and Other Models of Providence

Providence concerns all the ways God governs, manages, or *provides for* creation. This includes God's creating, sustaining, influencing, and interacting with creation. As one might expect, several models exist for how God exercises providence. In this section I describe six distinct models: theistic determinism, Molinism, open theism, timeless knowledge, simple foreknowledge, and process theism. I close with a comparative summary.

Theistic determinism. By "theistic determinism" I mean the view espoused by John Calvin and Jonathan Edwards according to which God is the ultimate sufficient cause of all events (Pereboom, 2011). To say that God is the *ultimate* cause of all events is to say that every causal chain starts with God. Whether God acts directly or through created intermediaries, behind every creaturely event is God's causal activity. To say that God is the *sufficient* cause of all events is to say that God's activity, whether direct or indirect, is always causally determinative. The course of events thus cannot in any respect deviate from God's intended outcome. For the theistic determinist, the whole history of creation – past, present, and future – meticulously plays out exactly as God wants it to and does so *because* God efficaciously causes it to play out that way. God's creative decree specifies a unique actual future (UAF), and God has exhaustive definite foreknowledge (EDF) of that UAF, simply by virtue of knowing his own causal contributions to creation. The future is causally, alethically, epistemically, and providentially settled. To the extent that there is creaturely freedom on this model, it is *compatibilistic* freedom, namely freedom compatible with determinism.[24] Finally, there are no initial constraints on what God can do with creation other than ones that are intrinsic to the divine nature and therefore metaphysically necessary.

Molinism. Molinism is the view of Luis de Molina (1535–1600) according to whom God creates based on *middle knowledge*, namely nonnatural, prevolitional know-ledge of conditional future contingents (Flint, 1998). Such knowledge is *nonnatural* because it is independent of God's nature. It is *prevolitional* because it is independent of God's will. The content of God's middle knowledge thus comes from outside God, so to speak, and before (in the explanatory order) God decides what sort of world, if any, to create. It therefore places an extrinsic and metaphysically contingent constraint on what God can do with creation. By middle knowledge, God knows what outcome *would* result from *any* logically possible causally specified

---

[24] I take "determinism" here to be *inclusive* of God's primary causal activity. So I regard McCann (2005) as a "compatibilist" about determinism because he's a compatibilist at the primary causal level despite being an incompatibilist at the secondary causal level.

creaturely indeterministic scenario.[25] Such scenarios include, but are not limited to, those involving creaturely libertarian free choices. Suppose, for example, that in some indeterministic scenario Peter is free both to deny and not to deny Christ. According to Molinism, God knew explanatorily prior to his creative decision which of those outcomes *would* eventuate were God to create Peter and put him in that scenario. With this knowledge in hand, God meticulously decides which string of scenarios to bring about and thereby knows exactly how things will play out *without* having to be the ultimate sufficient cause of all events. The future is causally open, but alethically, epistemically, and providentially settled.

Open theism. Open theism shares Molinism's commitment to a causally open future but rejects its controversial apparatus of middle knowledge. As with theistic determinism, the metaphysically necessary divine nature is the only initial constraint on what God can do with creation. Open future open theism believes the future is causally, ontically, alethically, epistemically, and providentially open because God wanted it that way. There is no UAF, and God does not have EDF. Rather, God knows the future as open-ended because it is open-ended. To manage an open-ended world, God does exhaustive contingency planning, wherein God considers every logically possible creaturely scenario – whether to allow it in the first place and, if he does allow it, how best to respond if it should come about. Contingency plans in place, God sets up the initial conditions and the causal system within which creatures operate and delegates some of his decision-making power to them. God's providence is thus not meticulous but *general.* God specifies only *some* of what comes to pass and leaves it to creatures to specify the rest.

Timeless knowledge and simple foreknowledge. Like Molinism and open theism, these models affirm a causally open future. Like open theism, both reject the Molinist apparatus of middle knowledge and thus affirm that God's providence is general and not meticulous. Unlike open theism, both affirm that God has EDF. So, the future is causally and providentially open but alethically and epistemically settled. To the extent that what happens in creation does not follow necessarily from God's causal activity (direct or indirect) God's EDF is based on the *actual occurrences* of creaturely events. On the timeless knowledge model, God exists timelessly and knows how the complete story of creation plays out because God "sees" the whole timeline from the vantage point of his timeless eternity. This model usually holds that the future is *ontically* settled (cf. Rogers, 2008). On the simple foreknowledge model, in contrast, God is not timeless but rather temporally everlasting. This model

---

[25] The scenario must be fully causally specified to ensure there are no hidden variables that might make it deterministic (Flint, 1998: 40).

usually holds that the future is ontically open. Nevertheless, proponents insist, in whatever way the future plays out, it has always been true that that's how it was going to play out, and so God, being essentially omniscient, has always known those truths (Hunt, 2001).

Process theism. Process theism shares open theism's commitment to general providence but goes much further. The future is causally, ontically, alethically, epistemically, and providentially open – not because God wants it that way, but rather because it's metaphysically necessary. God never had any choice about whether there would be a creation and whether it would be open-ended. On the process view, indeterministic freedom or "creativity" is a metaphysically necessary and pervasive feature of reality and so God *cannot* deterministically bring about anything in creation. God can act persuasively, or in an indeterministically influencing manner, but cannot act coercively, or in a way that unilaterally brings creaturely events about. The relation between God and creation on process theism is thus a kind of symbiosis in which God and creation both need each other. Creation needs God's guiding hand, for it has no intrinsic sense of direction and would become chaotic without God. God, in turn, cannot accomplish anything in the world without creaturely cooperation. Because of this symbiotic relationship, process theists reject creation ex nihilo and view God and creation as co-necessary and coeternal aspects of a world process. At every stage, God's activity is constrained by the *prior* state of the world process.[26]

To finish comparing these models it is helpful to introduce some conceptual distinctions. First, concerning the *specificity* of divine providence, a model may hold that God's creative decree specifies all creaturely events (theistic determinism and Molinism), some creaturely events but not others (open theism, timeless knowledge, and simple foreknowledge), or no creaturely events (process theism). The issue here is whether God's creative decree settles the entire course of creation history, or rather leaves the future partly or wholly open-ended. If a model holds that God specifies all creaturely events, I say it affirms *meticulous* providence. If a model holds that God specifies at most some creaturely events, I say it affirms *general* providence.

Second, concerning the *manner* of divine providence, a model may hold that God's causal activity toward creation is always determining (theistic determinism), only sometimes determining (Molinism, open theism, timeless knowledge, and simple foreknowledge), or never determining but always at most nondeterministically influencing (process theism).

---

[26] Although process theism isn't minimally monotheistic as I defined that notion, I include it here for contrast and to make clear that, even though open theism and process theism have considerable overlap, they represent two fundamentally different models of divine providence.

Third, concerning *constraints* on divine providence, a model may hold either that God's (initial) creative options are constrained by factors extrinsic to the divine nature (Molinism and process theism) or unconstrained by any such factors (theistic determinism, open theism, timeless knowledge, and simple foreknowledge). For Molinism, middle knowledge constrains God's creative options. God cannot bring about any world incompatible with his middle knowledge. For process theism, what God can do with creation is always already constrained by the prior state of the world process.

Fourth, concerning the *type of world* God has created, a model may hold that the world is deterministic and therefore that creaturely freedom (to the extent it exists) must be understood as compatible with determinism (theistic determinism), or a model may hold that the world is in some respects fundamentally indeterministic and that creaturely freedom (to the extent it exists) should at least sometimes be understood in a way that is *in*compatible with determinism (Molinism, open theism, process theism, timeless knowledge, and simple foreknowledge).

Fifth and finally, a model may affirm that God has EDF (theistic determinism, Molinism, timeless knowledge, and simple foreknowledge) or deny that God has EDF (open theism and process theism).

Table 1 summarizes the preceding distinctions. Theistic determinism and process theism occupy opposite ends of the spectrum when it comes to God's power over creation. Theistic determinism says that God unilaterally determines everything in creation, whereas process theism says that God does not and cannot unilaterally determine anything in creation. Molinism, timeless knowledge, simple foreknowledge, and open theism occupy the middle ground between those extremes. Molinism shares both theistic determinism's commitment to meticulous providence and process theism's affirmation of external constraints on God while affirming with open theism that God deliberately makes room for indeterministic creaturely freedom. Open theism shares with process theism a rejection of meticulous providence while affirming with theistic determinism that God's creative activity is externally unconstrained – God could have unilaterally determined everything but instead chose to make room for indeterministically free creatures. Timeless knowledge and simple foreknowledge are providentially equivalent to open theism,[27] but part ways with respect to whether God has EDF.

---

[27] This claim is defended by Sanders (1997) and Hasker (1989: ch. 3) but contested by Hunt (2009a). I agree with the former. Insofar as God's knowledge of what will happen in creation comes from the *actual occurrences* of creaturely events, that knowledge comes too late in the explanatory order for God to make providential use of it. Robinson's (2003: 211, 229–225) defense of an "Arminian" EDF model supports this. His model is equivalent to open theism with exhaustive contingency planning. He observes (p. 235), "neither model offers more divine control than the other."

Table 1 Models of divine providence compared

	Theistic determinism	Molinism	Timeless knowledge / Simple foreknowledge	Open theism	Process theism
Specificity of providence	Meticulous	Meticulous	General	General	General
God's activity toward creation	Always determining	Only sometimes determining	Only sometimes determining	Only sometimes determining	Never determining
Extrinsic constraints on God's (initial) creative options?	No	Yes	No	No	Yes
Creaturely moral freedom (to the extent it exists)	Always compatibilist	At least sometimes incompatibilist	At least sometimes incompatibilist	At least sometimes incompatibilist	Always incompatibilist
God has EDF?	Yes	Yes	Yes	No	No

2.4 A Brief History of Open Theism

Having defined what open theism is, from *mere* open theism to the bivalentist, ECP-affirming OFOT variant I endorse, I conclude this section with a summary of open theism's history.

The historical roots of open theism lie in two ancient ideas: (1) that there is future contingency, most importantly but not exclusively concerning human free choices, and (2) that future contingency is incompatible with the future's being alethically and/or epistemically settled. Add in theism, and you have all the essential ingredients for mere open theism.[28]

That there are future contingents, namely causally undetermined events, was widely accepted in antiquity. While there were those like the Stoics who held that everything is causally determined, many ancient scholars affirmed future contingency (Boyd, 2010). As for the idea that future contingency is incompatible with an alethically and/or epistemically settled future, that seems to have been the view of Aristotle (*De interpretatione* 9), Cicero (*De divinatione* II.5–7), Epicurus (O'Keefe, 2005), Alexander of Aphrodisias (Sharples, 1983), and Porphyry (Den Boeft, 1970: 56), among others. In addition, as I argue in Section 3.1, several biblical passages suggest God faces a partially open-ended future. Nevertheless, the dominant views in early Christianity at least seem to have been variations on the simple foreknowledge and timeless knowledge views (Jorgenson, 1992).

The earliest documented open theist is a fourth-century Christian named Calcidius, known chiefly as a translator of Plato's *Timaeus*. There is some uncertainty regarding his dates, with some scholars placing him early in the fourth century and others placing him near the end (Gersh, 1986: ch. 6). In any case, Calcidius wrote a treatise on fate in which he affirms both future contingency and that God knows the contingent *as contingent* (Den Boeft, 1970: 52). In short, because the future is causally open, it is also epistemically open for God.[29]

Perhaps because he was not in a position of ecclesiastical authority, Calcidius's views did not catch on. By the time of Boethius (480–524), if not before, it had become standardly assumed that knowledge conforms to the mode of the knower and not to the nature of what is known. Consequently, God as a necessary being is somehow able to know the contingent as though it

---

[28] Mere open theism also requires that the future be providentially open, but this follows from its epistemic openness plus God's being a maximally excellent knower. Thus, if the future were providentially settled, it would also have to be epistemically settled since God would have EDF in virtue of knowing his own activity of having providentially settled everything. Hence, the future can be epistemically open for God only if it's also providentially open for him.

[29] For detailed assessment of Calcidius as an open theist, see Rhoda (2022). Was Calcidius an open theist?, http://alanrhoda.net/wordpress/2022/08/was-calcidius-an-open-theist.

were *necessary*, and thus can have infallible knowledge even of matters that remain in themselves contingent (Boyd, 2010: 44).[30]

Another early emergence of open theistic ideas occurs under Islam. While much of the Islamic tradition leans strongly toward theistic determinism, the Mu'tazilite school, which flourished from the eighth through tenth centuries, affirmed creaturely libertarian freedom to protect the justice of God in punishing sin. Toward the end of the Mu'tazilite period, Qadi `Adb al-Jabbar (c. 935–1024), speaking of divine omniscience, stays notably silent concerning God's knowledge of the future: "You know that He is omniscient of the past and present and that ignorance is not possible for Him. And you know that He knows everything that was, everything that is, and how things that are not would be if they were" (Lodahl, 2009: 59).[31]

In the context of Judaism, the most explicit early affirmations of open theism come from ibn Daud (c. 1110–c. 1180) and Gersonides (1288–1344). According to Rudavsky, ibn Daud held that, with respect to future contingents, "the most God knows is that such a thing is possible"; God does not know "which of the two possibilities will be actualized." And in response to the "sophist" who charges that this makes God ignorant, ibn Daud replies negatively that there is nothing determinate there to be known (Rudavsky, 2000: 125–126). Similarly, Gersonides held that God's foreknowing the outcomes of future contingencies is incompatible with their status as contingencies, so God cannot have such knowledge. Again, this is no defect in God's omniscience because perfect knowledge of contingencies is to know them as they are, that is, as contingent (Rudavsky, 2000: 132).[32]

Moving back to Christianity, during the late medieval period a series of thinkers beginning with Peter Auriol (c. 1280–1322) and including Walter Chatton (1285–1344), Arnold of Strelley (early–mid fourteenth century), Robert Holcot (c. 1290–1349), and Peter de Rivo (c. 1420–1499), criticized prevailing views on divine foreknowledge of future contingents and advocated for a kind of "semi-open" theism. They held generally that future contingency is incompatible with divine *fore*knowledge and even *fore*truth. Affirming future contingency, they thus affirmed the openness *of the future* but not, it would seem, the openness *of God*.[33] Auriol, in particular, held to absolute divine immutability, so he couldn't say that God knows the contingent as contingent, for that would imply change in God's knowledge as those contingencies

---

[30] For Boethius, see his *De consolatione philosophiae*, V.6.1. Calcidius rejects this idea on the grounds that it falsifies God's knowledge (Den Boeft, 1970: 52).

[31] For more on Islam and open theism, see Sanders, J. (n.d.). Muslim scholarship on open theism, https://drjohnsanders.com/muslim-scholarship-on-open-theism.

[32] Note the rejection of the Boethian idea that knowledge conforms to the mode of the knower and the return to the Calcidian idea that knowledge conforms to the nature of what is known.

[33] See Schabel (2000) for an analysis of these thinkers: chapters 2–6 for Auriol; chapter 10 for Chatton, Strelley, and Holcot; and chapter 12 for de Rivo.

resolved into settled actualities. Instead, he held that God unchangingly knows future contingencies "indistantly." It's not entirely clear what he meant by this negative characterization of God's knowledge. My conjecture is that Auriol and other semi-open theists were groping toward what we today call *content externalism*. The idea is that God is *intrinsically indifferent* to creation in roughly the way that a mirror is indifferent to what it reflects.[34] Nevertheless, God's mind, like the mirror, automatically takes the content of or "reflects" whatever is put before him. Thus, whatever happens in creation, as it happens, is reflected in and therefore extrinsically "known" by God without producing any change or variation in God.[35]

After de Rivo's condemnation by Pope Sixtus IV in 1473, Auriol-style semi-open theism died out, but open theism proper soon reemerged after the Protestant Reformation broke the Roman Catholic theological monopoly in the Christian West. Protestant expressions of open theism emerged slowly at first, but increased rapidly from the eighteenth century on, especially in Arminian and Wesleyan circles. Significant proponents include Samuel Fancourt (1678–1768), who wrote several treatises promoting and defending open theism around 1730; Adam Clarke (1762–1832), who published an influential commentary on the New Testament in 1831; Jules Lequyer (1814–1862), a French Catholic philosopher; and Lorenzo McCabe (1817–1897), who wrote two influential treatises promoting open theism around 1890. Today, while open theism remains a minority view, it has firmly established itself as a major player in philosophical and theological discussions of divine providence and foreknowledge.[36]

3 Support for Open Theism

Now that we have a solid understanding of what open theism is, we can profitably inquire whether it is true. In this section I look at reasons for affirming open theism over against its main monotheistic rivals. In so doing, I take minimal monotheism for granted. My contention is not that open theism is true all things considered, but that it is preferable to competing versions of minimal monotheism. I present both biblical and philosophical arguments for open theism. Regarding the former, since most of the discussion surrounding open theism has been conducted by people who take biblical authority very seriously, if it can plausibly be argued that the Bible

---

[34] Schabel (2000: 318) notes of de Rivo, who "adopted Auriol's position," "God is intrinsically indifferent to producing or not producing something outside of Himself."

[35] Schabel (2000: 101) notes of Auriol's position, "The indistant similitude ... abstracts from simultaneity, as well as from prior and posterior and the entire line of succession in time, in representing the existence of the future contingent as present, while it exists."

[36] Sanders, J. (2018). Who has affirmed dynamic omniscience and the open future in history?, https://drjohnsanders.com/affirmed-dynamic-omniscience-open-future-history.

teaches open theism, or at least a general model of providence, then that is a dialectically significant point in open theism's favor. Readers interested only in philosophical arguments may skip ahead to Section 3.2.

3.1 Biblical Support

I offer six lines of biblical evidence supporting open theism. I divide these into two groups, each comprising three lines of support. Passages in the first group suggest that God has exercised merely *general* and not meticulous providence. These passages thus suggest that the future is *providentially open*. As such, these passages pose problems for Molinism and theistic determinism, but not necessarily for the other models under consideration. Passages in the second group suggest that God faces an *epistemically open* future and therefore does not have EDF. These passages pose problems for all models under consideration apart from open theism.

In presenting these biblical considerations, I remind the reader that I am a philosopher and not a biblical scholar.[37] My contention is merely that the passages in question *plausibly* teach that the future is providentially and/or epistemically open and thus pose interpretive challenges for competing models. I do not claim that this evidence constitutes anything like conclusive support. That would take a much more thorough survey of the biblical evidence, both pro and con, than I can provide. Nevertheless, I think it fair to say that the positive case for thinking that the Bible teaches open theism is stronger than many nay-sayers realize. In Section 4.3 I look at some biblical arguments against open theism relating to prophecy and argue conversely that they aren't as strong as many critics think. At the end of the day, however, I doubt the debate can be settled on purely biblical grounds.

Divine epistemic receptivity. Several biblical passages suggest that God is epistemically receptive in the sense of receiving information from creation about matters that God has not already settled. For example, Genesis 2:19 says God brought all sorts of animals to Adam "to see what he would call them."[38] This suggests that God leaves certain details up to creatures to decide and thus that these details are not already specified in God's creative decree. This contrasts with meticulous providence, according to which *all* details of creation are specified in God's creative decree.[39] Other passages suggesting that

---

[37] For an example of biblical scholarship supporting open theism, see Fretheim (1984).

[38] All biblical quotations come from the English Standard Version.

[39] Following Feinberg (2001: 801–802), proponents of meticulous providence may try to blunt the force of such passages by distinguishing propositional from experiential knowledge and suggesting that God's creative decree only specifies *propositionally* what happens in creation without specifying what it's like for God to experience it happening. I think this response untenable. Because *all* possibility is ultimately grounded in God's nature, for God not to know

God receives information from creation include Psalm 14:2 ("The Lord looks down from heaven on the children of man, to see if there are any who understand, who seek after God.") and Genesis 18:21 ("I will go down to see whether they have done altogether according to the outcry that has come to me."). The phrases "to see if" and "to see whether" suggest that God doesn't already have this information *independently* of his consulting creation.

Adaptive providence. Several passages indicate that what God does is sometimes contingent upon what creatures do and thus that God adapts his providential dealings to creaturely contingencies. Jeremiah 18:7–10 says:

> At any time I might announce that a nation or kingdom will be uprooted, torn down, and destroyed. But if that nation I warned turns from its evil, then I will relent of the disaster I had planned to bring. And if at another time I announce that I will build up and establish a nation or kingdom, and if it does evil in My sight and does not listen to My voice, then I will relent of the good I had intended for it.

Note that even when God declares in seemingly categorical fashion that he "will" tear down / build up a nation, God reserves the right to reverse those declarations as changing circumstances warrant. A similar passage, Ezekiel 33:13–15, applies the same logic to individuals instead of nations.

Likewise, in the New Testament, regarding the coming of the "day of the Lord," Peter insists that God is "patient" and "not slow to fulfill his promise" and that we should live our lives in such a way as to "hasten" or speed up the coming of that day (2 Peter 3:9–12). If the complete timeline of creation is already settled, however, then how could we possibly speed things up? The passage suggests that the timing of the day of the Lord is flexible and thus not yet settled.

These passages make perfect sense on open theism, but they make poor sense on either theistic determinism or Molinism. Given meticulous providence, there is *zero* need for providential adaptation to creaturely developments because God's creative decree already and indelibly specifies all such developments. Why talk about adapting to contingencies one already knows for certain will never happen?

Divine disappointment and anger. God sometimes expresses disappointment over how his own plans turn out and is frequently depicted as feeling intense anger and sorrow when creatures sin. For example, in Genesis 6:5–6 it says God saw the great wickedness of man and "regretted that He had made man on the

---

in advance what it would be like for him (and for any possible creature) to experience any possible reality implies a failure of self-knowledge on God's part. Feinberg's proposal is thus implicitly a denial of God's epistemic perfection. *Pace* Feinberg, the distinction between God's merely imagining a possibility and experiencing its actuality is not a distinction of *content*, but of God's *intentional stance* toward that content.

earth" and "was grieved in His heart." Similarly, in Numbers 32:14 we are told that God had "fierce anger" against Israel, and in Deuteronomy 9:8 we are told that God was "so angry" with Israel that he was "ready to destroy" them. But if God exercises meticulous providence, then why would he ever become disappointed or angry since God always gets *exactly* what he has sovereignly decreed? On theistic determinism God not only specifically *wills* everything that happens in creation, he also ultimately *causes* it to happen. But then it seems that God's sorrow and anger (if God can truly feel them at all) could only be properly directed at himself since God alone is ultimately responsible for things turning out as they do. On Molinism God's creative options are constrained by middle knowledge, and so I can understand how God could feel *chagrin* over not having had better prevolitional options, but again, since God knowingly selected *this* creation history with all its negatives, I don't understand how God could feel intense sorrow or anger over creaturely outcomes he himself specifically decreed.

Divine testing and discovery. The preceding categories of passages are problematic for meticulous providence, but not for EDF per se. Models like simple foreknowledge that affirm only *general* providence are already committed to God's epistemic receptivity to creation. Similarly, passages describing God's adaptive providence can be understood as expressing God's *general* providential policies independently of what God specifically knows will happen. Finally, because general providence allows for events that God does *not* specifically intend but only *merely permits*, such models can readily make sense of God's feeling sorrow or anger when creaturely events run contrary to God's will.

Other passages, however, do pose problems for EDF because they suggest that the content of God's knowledge is not exhaustively definite but rather sometimes indefinite. One such category of passages involves divine testing. In Genesis 22:12 God says "now I know that you fear God" to Abraham after he passes the test of being willing to sacrifice Isaac. On the assumption of EDF we would expect God to say "I knew you would," not "now I know." The latter phrase suggests that something *became* definite or determinate about Abraham's character that was previously indefinite or indeterminate. That would explain why God *now* knows something he didn't know before – the information that Abraham will pass the test simply wasn't available until Abraham passed the test. Likewise, several other passages (e.g., Exodus 16:4; Deuteronomy 8:2; Deuteronomy 13:1–3; Judges 2:21–22; 2 Chronicles 32:31) explicitly say that God tests people to know *whether* something is the case or not (e.g., whether they will keep God's commandments). Again, if God had EDF, such testing would seem unnecessary. But if the process of testing renders determinate something that was previously indeterminate, then these expressions can be taken at face value.

Divine uncertainty. God is sometimes depicted as being uncertain regarding certain future events. In Numbers 14:11 and Hosea 8:5, for example, God poses seemingly nonrhetorical questions regarding *how long* certain conditions will last. If God has EDF, why would he pose such questions?[40] Similarly, in Ezekiel 12:3 God says to the prophet that "perhaps" the people will understand. Furthermore, in Exodus 4:8–9 God proposes a two-tiered contingency plan to Moses: "*If* they will not believe you or listen to the first sign, they *may* believe the latter sign. *If* they will not believe even these two signs or listen to your voice, you shall take some water from the Nile and pour it on the dry ground, . . . " (emphasis added). Again, if God has EDF, then why not just say "do these three signs and they will believe"? If God's goal is to instill confidence in Moses (cf. Exodus 4:1), then why hedge with unnecessary and counterproductive "ifs" and "maybes," unless God himself is uncertain whether one, two, or three signs will suffice?

Divine surprise. Finally, God sometimes expresses surprise when things don't turn out as he expected. In Isaiah 5:4 we read that God "looked for" or expected his vineyard (i.e., the Israelite nation) to yield good grapes, but it yielded wild grapes instead. Likewise, in Jeremiah 3:7 God says (again of the Israelite nation): "I thought, 'After she has done all this she will return to me,' but she did not return." In both cases, God seemingly expected something that didn't happen. This is easy to make sense of on open theism: There was a high objective probability that things would go a certain way. Knowing those probabilities, God expected things to go that way. When they didn't, God was surprised. Given EDF, in contrast, any surprise on God's part seems impossible, for God would have already known with absolute certainty how things would turn out. A straightforward reading of these passages, therefore, supports the idea that the future is epistemically open for God.

3.2 Philosophical Support

Compared to the biblical case for open theism, I believe the philosophical case to be nigh decisive. My contention is that, from among the minimally monotheistic models under consideration, *only* open theism, and more specifically only

---

[40] One might contend that these questions are rhetorical and anthropopathic, that is, they display God with human-like emotions as an accommodation to finite creaturely understanding. On that reading, God may be seen as *venting his frustration*, so to speak, by asking "how long." That seems like a plausible take to me, so I don't take these verses as strong evidence against EDF. The rhetorical reading, however, still poses a problem for meticulous providence as it's not clear how God could feel anything like frustration over details he has specifically decreed.

OFOT, can consistently accommodate future contingency. The core of my argument – call it the Open Future Argument (OFA) – runs as follows:

(1) There is future contingency in creation (i.e., the future is causally open).
(2) If there is future contingency in creation, then either thoroughgoing open futurism is true or preventable futurism is true.
(3) Therefore, either thoroughgoing open futurism is true or preventable futurism is true. (From 1 and 2)
(4) Preventable futurism is not true.
(5) Therefore, thoroughgoing open futurism is true. (From 3 and 4)

This argument is obviously valid, so its soundness turns on premises (1), (2), and (4). Over the next three sections I argue for each of those premises in turn. By "thoroughgoing open futurism" I mean the thesis that *there is no unique actual future* because, from among all the causally possible futures (which I assume to be a nonempty set), nothing singles out or specifies any one of them as *the* actual future. The upshot of OFA is that if the future is causally open, then it is open in *all five* senses discussed previously. More explicitly, if the future is causally open, then it is ontically, alethically, epistemically, and providentially open as well. If we combine thoroughgoing open futurism with minimal monotheism, then it follows that OFOT is the only game in town.

3.2.1 OFA Premise (1): Future Contingency in Creation

Future contingency is the idea that the future is, in some respects, causally open and that there is, therefore, *more than one* causally possible future. Future contingency entails causal indeterminism and so is incompatible with thoroughgoing causal determinism. The "in creation" qualifier renders premise (1) incompatible with theistic determinism.[41] When I speak of future contingency in what follows, I take that qualifier as a given.

I offer four arguments in favor of future contingency. The first three are relatively brief. The fourth is a more extended discussion of the problem of *moral* evil.

First argument: quantum mechanics. The interpretation of quantum mechanics is an incredibly difficult topic. There are several competing and, to the extent we can test these matters, empirically equivalent interpretations of quantum mechanics.[42] Some of these, such as the standard Copenhagen interpretation

---

[41] Theistic determinists can say that *God* retains indeterministic or libertarian freedom and thus, at that level, there remain future contingents, but theistic determinism rules out future contingency at the nondivine level of creation.

[42] Myrvold, W. (2022). Philosophical issues in quantum theory, https://plato.stanford.edu/archives/fall2022/entries/qt-issues.

and more recent collapse theories, are fundamentally stochastic or indeterministic. Others, like the de Broglie–Bohm pilot wave model, are deterministic. Since I don't want to enter into the complex debate of which is the "correct" interpretation, I will simply say that *if* one of the indeterministic interpretations is correct in a metaphysically fundamental way, then there are future contingents.[43] And, further, since *whether* one of the indeterministic interpretations is correct remains well within the realm of epistemic possibility (as far as the experimental evidence goes), that there are future contingents should be regarded as well within the realm of epistemic possibility. Obviously, I do not offer this as a strong argument *for* future contingency. Pressing that sort of argument would take me too far out of my depth. I merely offer this as a preliminary reason to take indeterminism and future contingency seriously.

Second argument: phenomenology. When faced with a choice between competing options, we typically *feel* like it is *up to us* which way we choose. In many cases such feelings may have little, if any, metaphysical import. More than we might like to admit, we are creatures of habit who tend to go with the flow according to whichever inclination is strongest at the moment. Put me in my favorite fast-food restaurant and, unless something upsets my normal volitional rhythm (like a really tempting special!), I'm going to order the same thing every time. My choice of entrée is compatibilistically free in that I take myself to have good reasons for my selection and don't feel externally pressured to make it, but I see no good reason to think it libertarianly or indeterministically free because I am not consciously choosing *not* to do otherwise. Indeed, thoughts of doing otherwise barely occur to me at all. But sometimes this feeling of up-to-usness points clearly toward a libertarian view of human freedom. This is especially so when we consciously deliberate about a choice because we are *torn* between the options. That is, we take ourselves to have strong but not nearly decisive reasons for each option, and the choice is one that matters to us, not something we can casually settle by, say, flipping a coin. In such cases, it feels like both options are causally possible for us and that *we* are the ones who tip the balance by establishing a preference ranking among the options that was not given to us by our reasons. While this isn't proof that we sometimes have libertarian freedom – a determinist can always posit subconscious factors that supposedly tip the balance – it is strong prima facie evidence for libertarian freedom.

---

[43] I add "in a metaphysically fundamental way" to sidestep McCann's (2005) view, according to which quantum indeterminism at most reveals causal contingency at the secondary or natural causal level, but not at the more fundamental primary or divine causal level. McCann's position amounts to a deterministic interpretation of quantum mechanics where God's primary causal activity plays the role of a hidden variable.

Third argument: moral responsibility. A commonly accepted moral principle is that *ought implies can*.[44] The idea is that if one never had the *intrinsic* power to act otherwise than one in fact does, then it makes no sense to suppose one *ought* to have done otherwise.[45] For example, it makes no sense to blame a person for not doing something physically or humanly impossible. Sometimes, however, moral responsibility hinges not on what one can do now, but on what one could have done earlier. For example, a long-time drug addict may not be able to resist taking another "hit" if offered one, but he can still be morally blameworthy for taking it if earlier in life he could have avoided going down the path toward addiction in the first place. So, to be more exact, we should say *ought implies can-or-could-have*. A closely related idea championed by Robert Kane is that moral responsibility requires that we be *ultimately responsible* for at least some of our choices. By "ultimate responsibility" Kane means that if we trace the causal ancestry of our choices back far enough, we eventually arrive at indeterministic "self-forming actions," ones for which we had unconditional (and intrinsic) power to do otherwise (Kane, 2005: ch. 11). Considering these ideas, it seems to me that even if moral responsibility is compatible with *some* of our choices being causally determined, it is not compatible with *all* of them being causally determined. If all our choices are causally determined, then we never have the intrinsic ability to do otherwise, for the causal forces at work always ensure that we do whatever we wind up doing. If all our choices are causally determined, then we are at most only *proximately* responsible for them and never *ultimately* responsible. We thus always have a perfect moral alibi – "The causal system made me do it!" – and so cannot be morally responsible for anything we do. Thoroughgoing determinism is therefore incompatible with human moral responsibility. Given that we have, and that future people will continue to have, moral responsibility, it follows that thoroughgoing determinism is false, that some human actions remain causally indeterministic, and thus that there is future contingency.

Fourth argument: moral evil. The problem of evil is a major challenge for every model of divine providence. The problem, simply stated, is that it seems highly plausible, at least initially, that if God is as good, powerful, and knowledgeable as minimal monotheists think, then the quantity, severity, and/or distribution of evils in creation should be significantly less than we observe. Because a comparative analysis of competing models of divine providence in relation

---

[44] The principle is usually attributed to Kant, *Critique of Pure Reason*, A548/B576.

[45] I say "intrinsic" power to act otherwise to sidestep Frankfurt cases wherein some kind of counterfactual intervention prevents one from *actually* doing otherwise even though, on one's own (i.e., intrinsically), one could have done otherwise.

to the *general* problem of evil would take us too far afield,[46] for current purposes I focus only on the problem of *moral* evil (i.e., sin) in relation to creaturely freedom. Moral evil occurs whenever morally free creatures behave badly by misusing their moral freedom.

A major reason why most models of divine providence affirm an indeterministic or libertarian conception of creaturely freedom – following Basinger (1996), I collectively call these models "freewill theism"[47] – is because such freedom is arguably *necessary* for defusing the problem of moral evil. If free creatures are the ultimate causal source of moral evil, as their having libertarian freedom implies, then creatures, not God, are ultimately to blame for the reality of sin. As creator, God is responsible for the *possibility* of sin, and remains in some sense an accessory to sin given that God could have reasonably (if not infallibly) anticipated and therefore prevented much (if not all) of it. But God, on all versions of freewill theism, is not causally responsible for the *actuality* of sin. God is not, in short, the author of sin. Morally free creatures are. Freewill theism thus allows one to *deflect* responsibility for moral evil away from God.

Furthermore, to counter the worry that a maximally good and powerful God could have and should have prevented many, if not most or all, actual sins, freewill theists can invoke various freewill theodicies to blunt the charge. According to one line of thought, God creates beings with significant libertarian freedom, and gives them considerable moral leeway with that freedom, because only such beings can autonomously develop their love for God and each other. In contrast, if God is the ultimate sufficient cause of all creaturely actions, as theistic determinism maintains, then creatures are ultimately, in effect, mere extensions of God's own will. Indeed, it's perhaps better to say that God creates libertarianly free creatures not primarily so that *they* can freely come to love God, but so that *God* can more fully love them. Mere extensions of God's will lack the kind of *alterity* or *otherness* from God that two human friends have with each other. An all-determining God could love us in roughly the same way we might, say, love a prized possession or a character in a novel we've written, but not in the way one loves an independent *person* precisely because we wouldn't have enough independence from God to be objects of love in that sense. As the saying goes, "If you love something, set it free." Plausibly, God has made us morally free because he wants a loving relationship with creaturely persons and not mere creaturely possessions.

---

[46] See Rhoda (2010), Rhoda (2022), and Hasker (2004) for discussion of how different models of divine providence fare with respect to the problem of evil.

[47] Freewill theism includes the Molinist, open theist, simple foreknowledge, and timeless knowledge models.

In contrast, if theistic determinism is true, then it's hard to see how one could meaningfully blunt the problem of moral evil. In the first place, there's no way even partially to deflect ultimate responsibility for moral evil away from God. Sure, given a compatibilist view of moral responsibility, a theistic determinist can argue that creatures remain *morally* "on the hook" for their sins despite being causally determined to do them. And by defending certain positions in meta-ethics (e.g., divine command theory), a theistic determinist can argue that God is *not* morally on the hook for creaturely sins despite being their ultimate sufficient cause. But there is no way for a theistic determinist to deny God's *causal* responsibility for the actuality of sin – well, not unless he denies that there is any moral evil.[48] In the second place, it is highly implausible on its face that an all-determining God could have sufficiently good reasons for causing all actual moral evil in the world, past, present, and future. Whatever reasons those might be, either God causes moral evil for its own sake (which would make God not maximally good) or God causes it for the sake of some greater good, one that necessitates nearly the same quantity, severity, and distribution of moral evils that we see. The problem with the latter option is that it's very hard to see why an all-determining God couldn't have achieved whatever greater goods he's aiming at without nearly as many, nearly as severe, and/or nearly as widespread moral evils. More specifically, the problem is not that we *don't understand* why a good God would cause so much moral evil, but rather that what we *do understand* (or think we understand) about goodness suggests strongly that a good God *would not* cause so much moral evil.[49] Even those who defend the idea that God *intends some* moral evil – a much weaker thesis than that God *causes all* of it – admit that it's counterintuitive (Hart & Hill, 2022: 6).

In sum, theists are much better off with respect to the problem of moral evil if they affirm creaturely libertarian freedom. Since libertarian freedom entails indeterminism and therefore a causally open future, the problem of moral evil gives theists a strong reason to affirm future contingency in creation, especially when taken in conjunction with arguments from quantum mechanics, phenomenology, and moral responsibility.

---

[48] White (2016) argues that because evil is a privation God cannot be *causally* responsible for sin. But this is a non sequitur. All that follows from the privation theory is that God cannot cause evil to exist *independently* of something otherwise good. It doesn't follow that God cannot cause evil to exist *in conjunction with* something otherwise good. If God is the ultimate sufficient cause of *all* events, then God is the ultimate sufficient cause of all morally evil events.

[49] I develop this line of thought more fully in Rhoda (2008) and Rhoda (2022). To the extent that the problem of evil is driven by what we think we *do* understand about goodness, a purely skeptical response to the problem of evil cannot succeed without encouraging moral skepticism.

3.2.2 OFA Premise (2): Open Futurism versus Preventable Futurism

To a first approximation, fatalism is the view that (a) there is a unique way the future is going to go and (b) there is now nothing that can be done to avoid it, or at least, nothing any *creatures* can do to avoid it. Given, further, that there can be no *noncausal* constraints on whether otherwise free creatures can avoid that unique future, and it follows that fatalism entails a denial of future contingency (Todd, 2023).[50] Future contingency, recall, is the idea that the future is causally open and that there is, therefore, *more than one* causally possible future. Inasmuch as fatalism entails a denial of future contingency, it entails that there is *exactly one* causally possible future, which future is therefore causally determined (Taylor, 1992: 55).[51] In sum, then, by "fatalism" I mean the doctrine that there is a unique actual future (UAF) that is *now-unpreventably*[52] going to occur in virtue of being causally determined to occur. Put in these terms, we see that only two substantive assumptions are needed to construct valid arguments for fatalism. They are simply (1) there is a UAF, and (2) the UAF is causally now-unpreventable. Let's call these the unique actual future (UAF) and unpreventability (NP) theses, respectively.

Concerning UAF, since the fatalist's conclusion is that there is only one causally possible future, which future is therefore inevitably going to ensue, the premises of any valid fatalistic argument must posit something that singles out a unique possible future as *the* actual one. Let's call that something a *future specifier*. For example, alethic arguments for fatalism (or for what is often misleadingly called "logical fatalism"[53]) begin by assuming or attempting to establish that there is a collection of truths about the future – a complete, true story of the future – that specifies how the future is going to go. For there to be such a story is for the future to be alethically settled. Alethic arguments for fatalism then attempt to show that if the future is alethically settled, then it must also be now-unpreventable.[54] Likewise, epistemic arguments for fatalism

---

[50] That there can be no such noncausal constraints is contested by Pike (1965: 35), Fischer (2016: 41), and Hunt (1999: 12, 17) but affirmed by Craig (1990: 42) and Todd (2023). Todd argues, convincingly to my mind, that the existence of noncausal constraints on *basic* actions would have the massively implausible consequence that some sort of "metaphysical force field" could noncausally prevent someone from performing a basic action she is causally able to do.

[51] More exactly, fatalism entails only that the future is *now* causally settled as a matter of contingent fact. It doesn't entail that the future always has been causally settled or that is it metaphysically necessary that it be causally settled. If there were causal contingencies in the past, they're all behind us now. Moving forward, there's only one causally possible future.

[52] The term "now-unpreventable" comes from Prior (2003: 45).

[53] The terms "logical fatalism" and "theological fatalism," while common in the literature, are misleading because they suggest that these are different types of *fatalism* when they are really just different *ways of arguing* for fatalism.

[54] As Todd (2023) points out, it takes a further step to get from mere now-unpreventability to the claim that the future is *causally* now-unpreventable (i.e., causally settled). But, he argues, that

(or for what is often misleadingly called "theological fatalism") posit a complete, infallibly *known* story of the future. Such a story is often thought to exist in the mind of God. For there to be such a story is for the future to be epistemically settled. Epistemic arguments for fatalism then attempt to show that if the future is epistemically settled, then it must also be now-unpreventable.

But clearly the mere existence of a future specifier, apart from other considerations,[55] is not enough to entail fatalism. A future specifier entails that the specified future *will* happen, but fatalism makes the stronger claim that it *must* happen in the sense of being causally now-unpreventable. To bridge this gap, a fatalist may observe that some facts are unquestionably *fixed* or causally now-unpreventable such that we no longer do, and perhaps never did, have any power to bring them about. Plausible candidates include the laws of logic, mathematical truths, the laws of nature, the basic principles of morality, and the actual past. The fatalist may then propose that the fixed facts, whatever they are, collectively constitute a future specifier. If so, then there is not merely a specified future (UAF) but an unpreventably (NP) specified future. From that, fatalism follows.

To show that fatalism follows from UAF and NP let's sketch out the reasoning. Given UAF, there is a future specifier, S, the existence of which entails a specific future, F, namely

(1) $\Box$(S exists $\supset$ F comes to pass).

Given NP, S is causally now-unpreventable, or such that it will obtain (or will have obtained) no matter which causally possible future eventuates. Using N(X) to stand for <In all causally possible futures, X>, we can write NP as

(2) N(S exists).

Since the entailment in (1) is also unpreventable – if it is logically necessary that S $\supset$ F, then there cannot be a future in which S obtains and F doesn't – we can rewrite (1) using the N operator:

(3) N(S exists $\supset$ F comes to pass).

Finally, we can represent the fatalistic conclusion:

(4) N(F comes to pass).

(4) says that all causally possible futures are F futures or, equivalently, that F is the only causally possible future.

---

step can be crossed by noting that there are no plausible noncausal accounts of now-unpreventability.

[55] I discuss these considerations in Section 3.2.3.

All that remains is to show that (4) follows from (2) and (3) in virtue of the following transfer of necessity principle:

(5) $[N(p \supset q) \wedge Np] \supset Nq$.

The validity of this principle can be established by comparison with transfer of logical necessity, namely $[\Box (p \supset q) \wedge \Box p] \supset \Box q$. The latter is an axiom in every standard system of modal logic, and for good reason: If *all* possible worlds are ones at which $p \supset q$ is true, and if *all* are ones at which p is true, then there are *no* worlds at which q is false. Exactly parallel reasoning underwrites (5) by substituting "causally possible futures" for "possible worlds." Hence, the inference from (2) and (3) to (4) via (5) is demonstrably valid.

We thus arrive at a sufficient condition for fatalism: Simply establish that there is a future specifier among the fixed facts. Since the inference from (2) and (3) to (4) is logically impeccable, anti-fatalists have but two options for rebutting any given instance of this fatalistic argument schema. The first is to deny UAF and therefore to deny that any future specifier of the posited type exists. This was Aristotle's response to the alethic argument for fatalism, in which a complete, true story of the future plays the role of the future specifier. To deny UAF in this context is to deny that there is any such story. The future, Aristotle would say, is not alethically settled, but alethically open. Likewise, in response to the epistemic argument for fatalism based on God's foreknowledge, one could deny UAF by denying God's existence, by denying or (like LFOT) restrictively qualifying God's omniscience, or by denying (like OFOT) that the content of an omniscient God's knowledge constitutes a future specifier. The future, on any of these responses, is not epistemically settled, but epistemically open. Analogous *open future* or UAF-denying responses can be given to any valid argument for fatalism.

The anti-fatalist's second option is to deny NP. This was Ockham's response to both alethic and epistemic arguments for fatalism (Ockham, 1983), and it is the response given by modern-day "dependence" theorists (e.g., Swenson, 2016; Wasserman, 2021). Ockham conceded to fatalism the existence of at least two future specifiers: (i) a complete, true story of the future and (ii) God's knowledge of such a story. Contra fatalism, however, Ockham maintained that because there is future contingency, the truth of that story and God's knowledge of it are still *preventable* in virtue of there being causally possible futures in which some things actually true about the future are not true and in which some things actually foreknown by God are not foreknown. Analogous *preventable future* or NP-denying responses can be given to any instance of this fatalistic argument schema.

To establish premise (2) of the OFA all that remains is to show that a consistent anti-fatalist must either be a thoroughgoing open futurist or a preventable futurist. By a *preventable futurist*, I mean an anti-fatalist who admits the existence of one or more future specifiers while holding that the existence of those specifiers is, nevertheless, preventable. In contrast, a *thoroughgoing open futurist* is an anti-fatalist who denies that there are any future specifiers, preventable or otherwise. So defined, these anti-fatalist positions are mutually exclusive and jointly exhaustive. Given the demonstrable logical validity of the fatalistic argument schema sketched previously, there are no other options. Hence, if there is future contingency, then either thoroughgoing open futurism is true or preventable futurism is true.

3.2.3 OFA Premise (4): Against Preventable Futurism

While preventable futurism (PF) may initially look like an effective anti-fatalist strategy, it runs into problems when we examine its metaphysical coherence. Preventable futurism says both (a) there is a complete, true story of the future (i.e., a future specifier) and (b) the content of that story is to some extent yet-to-be-decided, since it depends on how future contingencies turn out. But, to use an obvious analogy, if a story (a novel, say) is complete and in print, then how can parts of it remain to be decided? Isn't it too late for that? And if parts of the story remain to be decided, then isn't the story still in the process of being written? How, then, can it be complete? To state the problem another way, PF requires us to take both of two incompatible perspectives on the future *with full ontological seriousness*. On the one hand, it requires that we consider the future as a complete, determinate totality. It is from this perspective that PF affirms the existence of a future specifier. On the other hand, it requires that we consider the future as containing yet-to-be-resolved contingencies. My argument is that you can't have it both ways. Because they are mutually incompatible, only one of these two perspectives can be the objectively correct or "God's eye" perspective of the unrestricted existential quantifier. Whichever way you go, either future specifiers or future contingency must be relativized and thereby pushed aside. The upshot is that *PF is metaphysically incoherent*.

My argument for this conclusion is somewhat lengthy, but not particularly difficult to follow. I call it the Contingency Entails Openness (CEO) argument. After stating the argument, I walk through it and explain its key premises. After that, I return to the OFA, take stock of where my philosophical case for open theism stands, and respond to possible objections.

(1) Preventable futurism (PF) is true. (Assumption for reductio)

(2) If PF is true, then there are future contingencies and there exists a future specifier, S. (Definition of PF)

(3) If there exists a future specifier, then it includes information specifying the outcomes of all future contingencies if there are any. (Definition of a future specifier)

(4) There exists a future specifier, S. (From 1, 2)

(5) There are future contingencies. (From 1, 2)

(6) Therefore, S includes information specifying the outcomes of all future contingencies. (From 3–5)

(7) Future specifiers are ontologically dependent on the information they include.

(8) Information specifying the outcome of a future contingency is ontologically dependent on the actual occurrence of an event that resolves that contingency.

(9) Ontological dependence is transitive.

(10) Therefore, S is ontologically dependent on the actual occurrences of all future contingency resolving events. (From 6–9)

(11) The actual occurrence of a future contingency resolving event changes an indeterminate (open question) information state into a determinate (specified outcome) information state.

(12) The indeterminate and determinate information states associated with a future contingency resolving event are mutually incompatible.

(13) Information states that are mutually incompatible cannot be co-realized.

(14) Information states that cannot be co-realized can only be realized in temporal succession.

(15) Therefore, the indeterminate and determinate information states associated with a future contingency resolving event can only be realized in temporal succession. (From 11–14)

(16) Therefore, S cannot exist until *after* all future contingency resolving events have occurred. (From 10, 15)

(17) If all future contingency resolving events have occurred, then there are no future contingencies.

(18) It is false that all future contingency resolving events have occurred. (From 5, 17)

(19) Therefore, S does not exist. (From 16, 18)

(20) Therefore, S both does and does not exist. (From 4, 19)

(21) Therefore, PF is false. (From 1–20 by reductio)

Let's walk through the CEO argument. Premise (1) is assumed to set up a reductio ad absurdum. If it can be shown that preventable futurism (PF) entails a contradiction, then it follows that PF is false.

The first phase of the argument (premises 2–6), draws out several straightforward consequences of PF. If PF is true, then at least one future specifier exists. A future specifier, by definition, identifies a particular possible future as *the* actual one (i.e., the UAF). Future specifiers may reside in the causal structure of reality (causally settled future), the ontological structure of reality (ontically settled future), the existence of a complete, true, linear story of the future (alethically settled future), God's having EDF (epistemically settled future), and/or God's meticulously provident creative decree (providentially settled future). Whatever form a future specifier takes, if the future specified by it includes future contingencies, as PF supposes, then the future specifier – call it S – must contain *information* specifying the outcomes of all future contingencies. Why information? Because S's *content* entails the coming to pass of the particular future that it specifies.

The second phase of the argument (premises 7–10) contends that S must be *ontologically dependent* on the actual occurrences of all *future contingency resolving events*. Premise (7) says that future specifiers depend ontologically on the information they include. This should be obvious. A future specifier contains information that singles out the UAF. The *token identity* of the future specifier is bound up with that information. Change or eliminate any of that information and you have either a *different* future specifier (and a different UAF) or no specifier at all.

Premise (8) says that information specifying the outcome of a future contingency depends ontologically on an event that *resolves* that contingency. By a future contingency resolving event I mean one that settles which of the possibilities associated with that contingency comes about. For example, suppose I am about to make a libertarian free choice between vanilla and chocolate ice cream and that I cannot choose both. Prior to the choice it is causally possible that I choose chocolate *and* causally possible that I choose vanilla instead. Now suppose I go on to choose vanilla. That choice resolves the future contingency into a settled actuality. Once resolved, the future contingency is no more because one of the options (vanilla) has become actual and the other (chocolate) is no longer causally possible. Having chosen vanilla, I can't now have chosen chocolate instead (on that occasion).

Now, I say that future specifiers are *ontologically* dependent on the actual occurrences of future contingency resolving events because ontological dependence is a type of explanatory dependence whereby the *existence* of something is explained. With that in mind, consider Figure 1.

If it is a future contingency whether I choose chocolate or vanilla ice cream, and if it is causally necessary that I do *exactly one* of those two things, then the set of causally possible futures partitions into vanilla futures $\{f_{v1}, f_{v2}, \ldots\}$ and chocolate futures $\{f_{c1}, f_{c2}, \ldots\}$. Since a future specifier entails the coming to pass of its corresponding future, if a future specifier exists, then it specifies either a vanilla future or a chocolate future and so is either a "vanilla specifier" $\{s_{v1}, s_{v2}, \ldots\}$ or a "chocolate specifier" $\{s_{c1}, s_{c2}, \ldots\}$. But since which type of future comes to pass – vanilla or chocolate – is *up to me* and is brought about in part by my free choice, which type of specifier exists – vanilla or chocolate – is also *up to me* and is

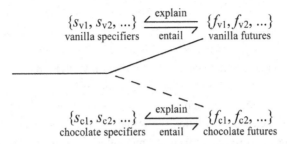

Figure 1 The structure of preventable futurism

brought about in part by my free choice. And, clearly, if something is brought about in part by my free choice, then it is explained in part by my free choice. The core of PF, therefore, is simply this: For any given future specifier, its existence is explanatorily dependent on, and brought about by, the actual occurrences of the future contingency resolving events that it specifies. And since it is the *existence* of the future specifier that is so dependent, this explanatory dependence is an onto-logical dependence.[56,57]

Premises (11)–(16) constitute the third phase of the argument, the burden of which is to establish that no future specifier can exist until *after* all future contin-gency resolving events have occurred. In other words, no future specifier can exist so long as there remains any future contingency. My argument, in a nutshell, is that the state of information explanatorily "before" a future contingency resolving event is *incompatible* with the state of information explanatorily "after" it.[58] Because of this incompatibility, this "before"/"after" sequence cannot be *merely logical*. It must be *temporal*.

To return to the ice cream example, explanatorily prior to my choice it remains an *open question* whether I choose chocolate or whether I choose vanilla. Both options are causally possible and neither is actual. The information state "before" my choice is thus an *indeterminate* one in which *either-V-or-C* is true but neither *V* nor *C* is true. Until I make my choice, it is true *that* one of those disjuncts comes to pass, but it remains undecided *which* of those disjuncts comes to pass. Explanatorily posterior to my choice, however, the situation has changed. The chosen option has become actual and the other is no longer causally possible. The information state "after" my choice is a *determinate*

[56] Finch and Rea (2008) make a similar point. On ontological dependence, see Tahko and Lowe (2020). Ontological dependence, https://plato.stanford.edu/entries/dependence-ontological.

[57] That ontological dependence is transitive (premise 9) should be obvious. If A could not exist were it not for B, and if B could not exist were it not for C, then clearly A could not exist were it not for C.

[58] I put quotes around "before" and "after" because I do not *assume* the sequence must be temporal. I am arguing that it must be temporal.

one in which V is true and C is false. The open question has been definitively answered by information introduced by my choice. I create the information *that I choose vanilla over chocolate* (on this occasion) by making the choice that I do. Had I not made that choice, that information would not have existed.

Now, obviously, it can't both be indeterminate which option comes to pass and determinate that *this* one comes to pass. Accordingly, the indeterminate ("before") and determinate ("after") information states associated with a given future contingency resolving event are mutually incompatible. Since mutually incompatible states cannot be co-realized on pain of contradiction, if one obtains simpliciter, then other does not. The only alternative is to *relativize* at least one of them. We could, for example, relativize the information states associated with a future contingency resolving event to *perspectives*. If it is indeterminate whether I choose chocolate or vanilla, then from the perspective of that information state, the information that I choose vanilla *does not exist*, whereas from the perspective of the determinate information state consequent upon my choice, that information *does exist*. Objective existence, however, isn't perspectival, unless we're talking about the all-encompassing "God's eye" perspective of the unrestricted existential quantifier. And PF regards both existence claims as objective. It says both *there is* a future specifier, one that includes all determinate information states consequent upon all creaturely free choices, and *there is* future contingency and thus there remain unresolved open questions as to *which* future comes to pass and *which* future specifiers exist. Given that both perspectives / information states are equally objective, their incompatibility means that they cannot coexist. They can only obtain in *temporal* succession. Hence, no future specifiers can exist until *after* all future contingency resolving events have occurred.

The fourth and final phase of the CEO argument (premises 17–20) wraps up the reductio against PF by deriving an explicit contradiction. If, as I have argued, no future specifiers can exist until after all future contingency resolving events have occurred, and if (per PF) it is not the case that all future contingency resolving events have occurred – because otherwise there would no longer *be* any future contingency – then it follows that no future specifiers exist. But PF says one does exist. So, PF is false.

3.2.4 OFA Recap

Having finished my explication of the Open Future Argument (OFA) and my defense of its key premises, I now consider its relevance to the various models of divine providence.

Premise (1) of OFA says that there is future contingency in creation. This premise is a direct challenge to theistic determinism. I defended this premise by appealing to quantum mechanics, the phenomenology of choice, moral responsibility, and the problem of moral evil.

Premise (2) of OFA says that if there is future contingency in creation, then either thoroughgoing open futurism is true or preventable futurism is true. This premise is a direct challenge to Molinism. I defended the premise, recall, by constructing a demonstrably valid fatalistic argument schema. Because the schema is valid, anti-fatalists must deny one of the premises. Open futurists deny premise UAF, which posits the existence of a UAF-identifying future specifier. Preventable futurists affirm UAF but instead deny NP by holding that the future specifier's existence is explanatorily dependent on the actual occurrences of future contingency resolving events. Despite its pretentions to the contrary, Molinism entails fatalism because it precludes *both* anti-fatalist strategies. It precludes open futurism because it straightforwardly posits a future specifier, namely, the content of God's meticulous providential decree. Molinism also precludes preventable futurism because it requires that information about how future contingencies turn out be available to God *independently* of the actual occurrences of those events. More fully, because middle knowledge specifies how any contingency *would* resolve in any causally specified creaturely indeterministic scenario in which that contingency obtains, and because this knowledge is available to God prevolitionally, namely independently of whether any creaturely events ever exist, middle knowledge information cannot come *from* the actual occurrences of future contingency resolving events.

Finally, premise (4) of OFA says that preventable futurism is false. This premise is a direct challenge to the simple foreknowledge and timeless knowledge models (and to Ockhamists / dependence theorists). It is also a challenge to limited foreknowledge open theism (LFOT). I defended this premise with the CEO (Contingency Entails Openness) argument.

One upshot of OFA is that *none* of the minimally monotheistic alternatives to open future open theism (OFOT) are tenable. If there is any future contingency, then the future must be open, not just from God's subjective perspective (LFOT) but objectively. Given future contingency and minimal monotheism, open theism (i.e., OFOT) is the only game in town.

Another upshot of OFA, and particularly the CEO subargument, is that if there is any future contingency, then there cannot *be* any future specifiers and therefore there cannot *be* a UAF. This means that if the future is causally open, then it must be ontically, alethically, epistemically, and providentially open as well.[59]

---

[59] This confirms, among other things, that an eternalist ontology of time entails fatalism *pace* Rogers (2008).

3.2.5 Objections Considered

I wrap up Section 3 by considering common objections to *future contingency incompatibility arguments*, of which OFA/CEO is an instance. These are arguments to the effect that future contingency is incompatible with the existence of future specifiers of one sort or another.

First, some think all such arguments inevitably commit a "modal fallacy" by either conflating what *will* happen with what *must* happen or by conflating necessity of the consequence with necessity of the consequent.[60] Undoubtedly, some incompatibility arguments are fallacious in this way, but OFA is not. Premise (2) of OFA is supported by a fatalistic argument schema that is demonstrably valid. Moreover, there is no *will*/*must* conflation, as my argument is not semantic, but metaphysical. I've argued that there cannot *be* any future specifiers so long as there *is* future contingency.

Second, some argue that because future specifiers of certain sorts are *not causal* they cannot be incompatible with future contingency. Augustine, for example, says that simply knowing something will happen cannot make it happen. He contends, therefore, that God's having EDF (an epistemic future specifier) poses no threat to future contingency (*De libero arbitrii* III.4). Likewise, it may be urged that neither alethic nor ontic future specifiers are causal. Neither its being true that something will happen nor its actual happening at a future temporal location can make it happen. Indeed, the latter would require the metaphysical absurdity of an event being causally prior to itself. Less clear is whether a providential future specifier can avoid being causal. Molinists would answer affirmatively, whereas most non-Molinists would disagree. In any case, a causal future specifier (i.e., a deterministic causal system) obviously must be causal. So, some types of future specifiers are causal, and others aren't. Regarding the *noncausal* ones, then, are Augustine and others correct in thinking that these cannot be incompatible with future contingency? Not at all, for it may well be that noncausal future specifiers *can only exist if* a causal future specifier exists (Todd, 2023).[61] That, in fact, is exactly what my CEO argument purports to show.

Third, many scholars from Boethius to the present seem to think that any apparent conflict between God's having EDF and future contingency can be solved by appealing to God's transcendence (e.g., McCann, 2005). The idea is that because God is in some sense "above" or "outside" time and interacts with creation solely via "vertical" or primary causation, God can know all that ever comes to

---

[60] For example, Schwartz, N. (n.d.). Foreknowledge and free will, https://iep.utm.edu/foreknow.
[61] As Edwards (2009 [1754], II.12) noted, "Infallible Foreknowledge may prove [i.e., entail] the [causal] Necessity of the event foreknown, and yet not be the thing which causes the Necessity."

pass from a transcendent standpoint without infringing on human freedom and future contingency. In response, while this is an effective response against incompatibility arguments that *assume* divine temporality (e.g., Pike, 1965), my argument doesn't do that. I make no assumption that preventable future specifiers must be temporally or otherwise immanently situated. My argument runs at the *ontological* level corresponding to the absolute or "God's eye" perspective. Given the ontological dependence of a future specifier on the actual occurrence of a future contingency resolving event, it follows straightforwardly that the future specifier must *itself* be a future contingent (Rhoda, 2014: 266–267). After all, if there exists a future specifier and if it is now up to me whether to choose chocolate or vanilla, then just as there is a causally possible future in which I choose chocolate and a causally possible future in which I choose vanilla, there is correspondingly a causally possible future in which a "chocolate specifier" exists and another causally possible future in which a "vanilla specifier" exists instead. Which type of future specifier exists is therefore just as much a future contingency as the outcome of my choice. And since future contingency is an inherently temporal status, it follows that no preventable future specifier can be atemporal. The transcendence response to future contingency incompatibility arguments thus ultimately fails to take future contingency seriously. Relativizing and immanentizing future contingency reduces it to a merely *as if* status. That is, from our immanent, situated perspective it seems *as if* there is future contingency, whereas from a fully objective, "God's eye" perspective there isn't any. To persuade themselves that their solution works, proponents of this response must engage in repeated "perspective toggling," considering matters transcendently when they want to affirm a UAF and immanently when they want to affirm future contingency. Open futurists refuse to play this conceptual game by dropping the assumption that there is a UAF and by holding that the transcendent perspective is *also* a temporal perspective.[62]

Fourth and finally, some may wonder why we need explanatory *cum* ontological dependence. Isn't *counterfactual dependence* enough to show, for example, that EDF is compatible with future contingency (Plantinga, 1986)? To return to my ice cream example, even though I chose vanilla, if I had chosen chocolate, then God would have always known I was going to choose chocolate. Is that enough to render God's knowledge sufficiently responsive to accommodate future contingency? Not hardly. While the ontological dependence of future specifier S on future event E licenses a counterfactual, namely,

---

[62] In Rhoda (2014: 265–266), I argue that if God is free in a way that leaves him "open options," then God has choices to make. But choices are essentially temporal events because they require a transition *in the chooser* from a not-having-yet-decided state to a having-decided state. So, if God makes choices among open options, then God must be temporal independently of creation.

<If E were not to occur, then S would not have existed>, ontological dependence is *not reducible* to counterfactual dependence. Indeed, ontological dependence is transitive (and typically asymmetric and irreflexive), whereas counterfactual dependence is nontransitive[63] (and sometimes symmetric and/or reflexive). Moreover, if ontological dependence were reducible to counterfactual dependence, then preventable futurism would completely fail as a counter to fatalism. After all, fatalists themselves would insist that future specifiers are counterfactually dependent on the events they specify. It follows from theistic determinism, for example, that if (counterfactually) I were to choose chocolate over the divinely predestined vanilla, then God would have foreknown (because God would have predestined) that I was going to choose chocolate. The presence of a counterfactual arrow running from future events to a future specifier is thus fully compatible with the fatalist's insistence that no relevant explanatory arrows run in that direction.

4 Challenges for Open Theism

In this section I reply to four common challenges facing open theism. Challenges one and two are primarily philosophical. The first is metaphysical, namely, that the God of open theism fails the test of perfect being theology. The second is ethical, namely, that the open theistic model of providence is too risky and so God ought not govern the world as open theists think he does. Challenges three and four are primarily theological and are usually situated within the context of a specific theological tradition, such as Judaism, Christianity, or Islam. The third challenge is that open theism cannot make adequate sense of scriptural prophecy. The fourth is that open theism is too far outside the theological mainstream to merit consideration by adherents of the tradition in question.

In what follows I pose each challenge as forcefully as I can and argue that open theists have the resources to meet the challenge. Open theism, I submit, is far more defensible than many of its critics realize.

4.1 It Diminishes God! The Challenge of Perfect Being Theology

Many critics believe open theism presents a diminished view of God, namely that it portrays God as *less great* than how God ought to be portrayed. According to perfect being theology (PBT), God is the greatest metaphysically possible being. PBT uses this idea heuristically to evaluate competing models of

---

[63] Lewis (1973: 32–35).

God. If God-according-to-model-A is clearly less great than God-according-to-model-B then, all other things equal, model B should be preferred.

To compare models of God in a way that doesn't degenerate into subjective "my God is bigger than your God" chest thumping, PBT focuses on "great-making" properties or attributes that are widely agreed to contribute to a being's overall intrinsic greatness, all else being equal (Nagasawa, 2017: 53–55). One such property is internal consistency. The greatest metaphysically possible being must, after all, be *possible*. If a model of God is internally inconsistent, that excludes it from consideration. Other properties generally regarded as great-making include necessary existence, power, goodness, personhood, knowledge, and wisdom. Obviously, to compare models of God with respect to some list of great-making properties, we must first satisfy ourselves that the properties in question belong on the list. This is often a matter of dispute.[64] Nevertheless, once we have an agreed list of great-making properties and are satisfied that those properties, individually or in combination, don't generate internal inconsistencies, there are two types of tests we can apply: extensive and intensive. Model A is *extensively superior* to model B just in case God-according-to-A has some great-making property that God-according-to-B lacks. Model A is *intensively superior* to model B just in case God-according-to-A possesses some degreed great-making property more fully than God-according-to-B does (Nagasawa, 2017: 56–57). In essence, PBT encourages us to think of God as having all possible great-making properties, each to the greatest degree possible, subject only to the constraint of internal consistency. To use PBT against open theism, therefore, one must either show that open theism is internally inconsistent or produce a competing model that is (a) internally consistent (as best we can tell), (b) either extensively or intensively superior to open theism with respect to some great-making property, and (c) neither extensively nor intensively inferior to open theism with respect to other, equally or more important, great-making properties. There are, obviously, many ways to press such a challenge. I reply to the most common.

Absolute simplicity. Classical theists argue that for God to be the greatest possible being he must be wholly independent of anything else and therefore must be *absolutely simple*, having no internal complexity. The thought, roughly, is that if God had any internal complexity, then God would be internally composed of more fundamental metaphysical constituents upon which he would ontologically depend.[65] Furthermore, if God is absolutely simple, then

---

[64] For example, classical theists like Dolezal (2011) argue that absolute divine simplicity, absolute immutability, and absolute impassibility are great-making attributes that God must have, whereas nonclassical theists like Mullins (2016) disagree.

[65] Vallicella, W. F. (2019). Divine simplicity, https://plato.stanford.edu/entries/divine-simplicity.

he cannot possess any unrealized potentiality in addition to his actuality and so must be absolutely immutable and impassible as well. Since open theists deny absolute divine simplicity, immutability, and impassibility, as argued in Section 2.1, open theism (so the charge goes) presents a diminished God compared to classical theism.

The first thing to note is that this objection targets not merely open theism but any nonclassical model of God that denies absolute divine simplicity, immutability, and/ or impassibility. That includes the simple foreknowledge and timeless knowledge models, as well as some versions of Molinism and theistic determinism.

Second, nonclassical theists can push back and challenge classical theism's underlying metaphysical framework. Arguments for absolute divine simplicity typically presuppose (a) that all internal complexity is compositional, (b) that composition needs a concurrent sustaining cause, (c) that the concurrent sustaining cause must be extrinsic, and (d) that this explanatory sequence cannot be infinite.[66] One can challenge (a) by opting for a relational rather than a constituent metaphysics (Wolterstorff, 1991). One can challenge (b) by affirming existential inertia, according to which some complex things don't need a sustaining cause to persist (Schmid & Linford, 2023). One can challenge (c) by affirming that free creatures are, in some respects, self-movers (Effler, 1962). And one can challenge (d) by holding that there can be infinite causal sequences (Hume, 1990 [1779]: pt. 9). I regard (a), (b), and (c) as more vulnerable than (d) but, in any case, derivations of absolute divine simplicity are not unproblematic.

Third and finally, nonclassical theists can play offense and argue that classical theism faces PBT problems of its own. For example, it can be argued that classical theism is explanatorily inadequate because it cannot make sense of metaphysical contingency. Suppose there is a contingent reality (creation). Either complete information about creation is intrinsic to God, or it isn't. If it is intrinsic to God, then, given absolute divine simplicity, that information is identical to God. And thus, because God exists necessarily, that information also exists necessarily. Consequently, we get a *modal collapse*: everything is necessary and nothing is contingent. If, however, that information is not intrinsic to God but extrinsic, then it follows from absolute simplicity that God is essentially and intrinsically *indifferent* to creation: God would be intrinsically the same even if there were no creation at all. But if that's right, then nothing *in God* can explain why there is anything contingent. The result is a radically nonprovidential God.[67]

---

[66] In his *Summa Theologica*, Aquinas employs each of these assumptions in arguing for divine simplicity. (b)–(d) occur in the "first way" argument of ST 1a.2, which concludes that God is purely actual. Aquinas uses that conclusion along with (a) to derive God's absolute simplicity in ST 1a.3.

[67] Schmid (2022) advances a similar argument.

This, I submit, implicitly undermines God's power, knowledge, and goodness – far more serious defects, if true, than anything the nonclassical theist faces by denying absolute simplicity.

Divine sovereignty. Some theistic determinists (e.g., Wright, 1996) believe all forms of freewill theism, and especially open theism, deny God's sovereignty by holding that God is not the ultimate sufficient cause of all events.

In response, being sovereign does not entail being all-determining. It merely entails that God is in charge, which open theists readily affirm. Indeed, open theists believe that, with respect to God's power, he could have created exactly the sort of world that theistic determinists believe God has created. The issue, therefore, is not *whether* God is sovereign and maximally powerful, but how God has chosen to *exercise* his power and sovereignty. According to open theists, God sovereignly chose *not* to be an all-determining micro-manager but chose, rather, to delegate some details of creation to his creatures. Furthermore, because God sets the ultimate causal parameters for creation, does exhaustive contingency planning, and can unilaterally intervene as needed, there is no possibility of events spinning out of God's control.

Divine transcendence. Another common charge is that, by denying God's immutability and timelessness, open theism compromises God's transcendence by, in effect, trapping God "in" time. And if time is a created thing, then God has become bound by creation and so is no longer transcendent.[68]

In response, open theists have two options. One is to reject the *container metaphor* of time and with it the idea that time is a created thing (Sanders, 2007: 202). To speak as if things can be "inside" or "outside" of time is to conceptualize time as a container of sorts. On this metaphor, all changes happen "inside" the container, and to be "outside" time is to be atemporal and immutable. But we need not conceptualize time in this way. On a relational view of time, time is neither a container-like "thing" nor a created thing but is merely the fact that *things change*. In short, time is real becoming. If reality from a "God's eye" perspective is dynamic and therefore changing, then time exists. And if God changes intrinsically in sync with a dynamic reality, then God experiences succession but is not "in" time. A second option is to take a Newtonian or substantival view of time and say that time is an aspect of God's inherently dynamic nature (Mullins, 2022). On this view time remains a container of sorts but is not created. Instead, God *is* the container. In short, God is not "in" time,

---

[68] "The critical weakness of open theism ... is its failure to properly grasp the divine transcendence, as disclosed by the doctrine of *creatio ex nihilo*." Kimel, A. (2016). Open theism, eternity, and the biblical God, https://afkimel.wordpress.com/2016/11/14/open-theism-eternity-and-the-biblical-god.

but rather time is "in" God. Of these two options I prefer the first, but either allows open theists to avoid the idea that a temporal God is somehow bound by time and thus not transcendent.

Divine perfection. A closely related objection is that open theism, and any view that denies God's absolute immutability, undermines God's essential perfection. The main argument for this goes back to Plato (*Republic* 381b–c): It is impossible for an essentially perfect being to change either for the better or for the worse and since, allegedly, all change is either for the better or the worse, an essentially perfect being must be immutable. The flaw in this argument is that change need not be either for the better or for the worse. Indeed, *not changing* is sometimes clearly worse. A stuck clock that no longer tracks the passage of time is worse than one that changes in sync with time's passage. Likewise, a God whose knowledge changes in sync with a dynamic reality is better than a God whose knowledge is "stuck" so that it cannot track reality.

Omniscience. There are at least four versions of the omniscience objection. Each faults open theism for not attributing to God *enough* knowledge, knowledge that, by the critic's lights, God ought to have.

The first version says that open theism denies God's omniscience by holding that there are truths God doesn't know. This charge, however, only applies to LFOT. It has no force against OFOT, which holds that God perfectly knows *all* truths.

The second version alleges that the God of open theism *knows less* than he would *if* he had EDF, and that this makes open theism deficient (Hunt, 2009b: 266–269). But this either reduces to the preceding point about LFOT or it is question-begging. On LFOT God admittedly knows less than he would know if he knew all truths. That's a known theoretical cost of LFOT and the major reason why most open theists affirm OFOT. If aimed at OFOT, however, then the charge is question-begging because the objection is only meaningful if God *can* have EDF despite the causal openness of the future. But this is something open theists explicitly deny. If, as OFOT holds, it is *impossible* that the future be both causally open and alethically settled, then faulting the God of open theism for not having EDF makes no more sense than for a Molinist to argue that a simple foreknowledge God *knows less* on account of lacking middle knowledge. No theist who believes that middle knowledge is impossible should be impressed by that charge.

The third version of the omniscience objection attempts to turn open theistic arguments for the incompatibility of causal openness and epistemic settledness against the open theist. The argument is that, if God remains free with respect to how he manages creation, and if it is impossible for God to know the outcomes of *any* free choices in advance, then God cannot know which choices *he* will make in the future. And if divine freedom extends to the laws of nature, then

God can't even know what will happen by way of secondary causal necessity, for God can't know whether he will decide, say, to reverse gravity in the next two nanoseconds. This, so the argument goes, leads to almost complete divine ignorance about the future.[69]

The flaw in this argument is that it overlooks the importance divine *contingency planning* has for open theism. God can know what he's going to do in the future because God has *already* considered *all* future possibilities and decided how to deal with them. Moreover, because God considers *all* future possibilities – which he can do as the ultimate source of all metaphysical possibility – there's no chance that unanticipated possibilities might prompt God's revisiting those decisions. So, if God does exhaustive contingency planning and decides that some things (e.g., laws of nature) shall remain stable and unchanging until the eschaton, then God can be confident that that's how it will be.

A fourth and final version of the omniscience objection is that, if open theism is true, then God has false beliefs and so isn't omniscient (Stewart, 2019). This objection can be supported by noting that belief pairs with expectation: If I expect event E to occur, then it is natural to say that I believe E will occur, or at least that I believe E will probably occur. As we have seen (Section 3.1), open theists cite biblical passages like Isaiah 5:4 and Jeremiah 3:7 to argue that God's expectations sometimes fail to be fulfilled. If expectations are beliefs, then it may seem that God had false beliefs.

In reply, even if we grant that expectations are beliefs, it doesn't follow that a failed expectation is a *false* belief. That follows *only if* we assume "retro-closure" (RC).[70] Given RC, if expected event E fails to occur, then it was previously true that E was *not* going to occur and thus *false* that E was going to occur. From an open futurist perspective, however, RC is a non sequitur. If E is a future contingent event with probability k of occurring, then what's true beforehand is neither <E will occur> nor <E will not occur>—for it remains an open question whether E occurs – but rather propositions like <E might-and-might-not occur>[71] and <E will-with-probability-k occur>.[72] E's eventual

---

[69] Versions of this objection are pressed by Kvanvig (2011: ch. 4) and Robinson (2003: 135–143).

[70] "Retro-closure" (RC) is Patrick Todd and Brian Rabern's term (Todd, 2021: ch. 7) for the thesis that $p \rightarrow PFp$, namely that if p is the case, then it always was the case that p will be the case. For example, RC says that if it rains on Tuesday, then it was true on Monday and all previous days that it was going to rain on Tuesday.

[71] I use "might-and-might-not" to express *causal contingency*, not mere epistemic contingency. To say E might-and-might-not occur is to imply that the objective chance of E's occurring is greater than zero and less than one.

[72] I hyphenate "will-with-probability-k" because the probability modifies *the strength of the expectation*, not its content. If you believe with certainty that the chance of event E's occurring is 0.9, then by the "principal principle" (Lewis, 1986b), the strength of your expectation or credence that E occurs should also be 0.9. This is not equivalent to your belief that *the chance of*

nonoccurrence only shows that *when the contingency resolves*, the latter two propositions *become false* (after having been true) and the *will not* proposition *becomes true* (after having been either false or neither-true-nor-false). Since God's knowledge perfectly tracks truth, when the contingency resolves, the content of God's beliefs changes accordingly. At no time, then, does God have false beliefs.

4.2 It's Too Risky! The Challenge of Divine Bodgery

Another common charge against open theism and any *general* model of divine providence is that it's *too risky*. A maximally good and powerful God *ought not* take the kinds of chances with creation that general providence supposedly entails. Sometimes the charge is simply that God's taking risks is unbecoming of divine perfection, making God like a cosmic gambler or "bookie than which none greater can be conceived" (Flint, 1990: 114). But the charge often takes on moral dimensions:

> [S]ince God couldn't know in advance whether humans would freely choose good or evil, God couldn't know in advance whether, over the long run, the actual world would be overall more good than evil. God thus engaged in a high-risk, high-stakes gamble. And if the gamble didn't play out well, the main victims would be the creatures rather than the Creator. . . . On the face of it, this doesn't seem consonant with divine goodness and wisdom. . . . Why should we think well of a God who plays a cosmic-scale game of roulette with the lives of his creatures? . . . Isn't a divine dice-thrower the epitome of irresponsibility? (Anderson, 2019: 227)

To strengthen the objection let's reflect on the potential stakes of God's "gamble." If libertarian free choices are required for humans to participate in God's kingdom, then it was antecedently *possible*, even if highly improbable, that all or nearly all humans would refuse to partner with God. In short, creation could have gone to hell in a handbasket (Grössl & Vicens, 2014). Indeed, *all* divine plans involving free creaturely choices could have gone awry due to creaturely non-cooperation. To use a Christian example, what if the incarnation had been thwarted by Mary's refusal to become Jesus's maternal vessel?[73] Or what if the biblical authors had decided not to write what God wanted? Should general models of providence undermine our confidence in the reliability of

---

E's occurring is 0.9 for, as we've supposed, you believe the latter with *certainty* and thus with a credence of 1.0. As Todd (2021: 145) notes, will-probably claims cannot be decomposed into nested futurative, F(), and probability, Pr(), operators as in $F(Pr(p))$ or $Pr(F(p))$ without semantic distortion. The exact sense is hard to capture in English; hence, the hyphenated phrase.

[73] Eastern Orthodox theologian Vladimir Lossky (1978: 89) writes: "Mary remained free to accept or to refuse. The whole history of the world, every fulfillment of the divine plan, was dependent on this free human response."

Scripture?[74] Furthermore, there is the problem of compounding contingencies. If God's plans depend on sequences of probabilistic events (e.g., strings of human free choices), then it's hard to see how God could reliably achieve those goals. Even if every individual event probability is high, when multiplied together the resultant compound probability can quickly become very low. In sum, on a general model of providence it seems that many of God's aspirations for creation could have come to naught and yielded nothing but suffering creatures in their wake. Is that worth the risk?

To rebut this objection, we need to reflect on the ethics of risk-taking in general, the nature of God's creation project, the nature of creaturely freedom, and God's resources for managing risk.

Regarding the ethics of risk-taking, five points deserve mention. First, there is nothing per se bad about taking risks, as pejorative terms like "gambler" and "bookie" suggest. Indeed, for creatures at least, risk-taking is unavoidable and often commendable. We rightly praise a hard-working entrepreneur or athlete who strives for a worthy, yet uncertain goal. Virtues like courage likewise require striking a balance between excessive risk-taking (foolhardiness) and excessive risk-avoidance (cowardice). Second, while there is nothing per se bad about risk, there is nothing per se good about it either. Sane and moral people don't take risks for their own sake, but for the sake of goods they believe those risks make possible (Hansson, 2013: 117). As the saying goes, "nothing ventured, nothing gained." Risks are sometimes warranted for the sake of potential gain. Third, the degree of risk for all affected parties should be proportionate to the potential gain. We can understand this, roughly, in terms of *expected value*: the sum of the value-weighted probabilities of the various possible outcomes should be *nonnegative*. Otherwise, one risks more than necessary without compensatory increase in potential gain. Fourth, to avoid unwarranted "collateral damage," we can't just look at the possible end results when assessing risks. We must consider the costs and benefits that might be incurred along the way and strive to ensure that gains for some interested parties don't involve unwarranted and uncompensated costs to others. In short, we should consider the impact of risk upon *all* parties potentially concerned (Hansson, 2013: 102–103). Fifth and finally, warranted risks should remain defensible in retrospect. Even if things turn out poorly, one should be able to look back and say, given the circumstances at the time, it was a good decision to have made (Hansson, 2013: ch. 4).

To illustrate, consider the *parenthood analogy*. While there are undoubtedly circumstances in which pursuing parenthood is ill-advised because of excessive

---

[74] Cf. Leithart (2004).

risk, most often it is a noble and worthwhile pursuit *despite* the risk involved. Even the best of parents under the best of circumstances cannot guarantee their kids turn out well. They cannot ensure their kids remain safe from all external threats, and they cannot ensure their kids never make foolish and self-destructive choices. Still, most parents would say the risks are worth it, not just for themselves, but for their kids, even though the latter could not have consented to the risks in advance. Similarly, God is not a cosmic gambler casually playing roulette with creaturely lives at stake. God is like a loving parent who, having carefully counted the potential costs of bringing morally free creatures into being and having fully considered the pros and cons of every possible providential arrangement and every possible creaturely contingency, decided to go ahead with it, knowing that, even if things should go poorly despite his providential efforts, it was still *worth it*, not just for God, but for *each and every* free creature to have had the opportunities it did.

Concerning the nature of God's project, how we assess divine risk-taking depends on what precisely God wants from creation. Pursuing any goal requires both a target (*what* one is aiming for) and a method (*how* one aspires to hit the target). Targets may range from highly specific (small target) to very generic (big target). As in archery, the smaller the target, the more the control required to hit it. Conversely, the bigger the target, the less the control needed. Smaller targets constrain one's methods more than bigger targets do. One may also aim at multiple targets simultaneously, some small, some big – my smaller, short-term target of finishing this paragraph is part of my larger, longer-term target of finishing this manuscript. With respect to divine providence, then, God may have both specific and generic goals. The more generic God's goals, the less control God needs to achieve them. If all of God's goals, or at least all of God's *central* goals, are generic,[75] then God doesn't need meticulous providence. God can selectively exercise more control when needed and less when it's not. The central worry behind the "it's too risky" objection – that a nonmeticulously provident God thereby lacks the degree of control needed to "hit" his targets while avoiding unjustified collateral damage – is thus invalidated. If God's central goals are good ones (as God's maximal goodness requires) and are somewhat generic, then God does not need a meticulously controlling method to reach his targets.

Suppose, for example, that salvation is corporate, not individual.[76] God offers salvation to everyone and ensures that everyone has a fair chance freely to accept or reject the offer (perhaps by giving post-mortem opportunities to those

---

[75] This is, roughly, what Rissler (2006) proposes.
[76] For biblical defense of this position, see Klein (2015).

who wouldn't otherwise have had a fair chance). Moreover, God does not elect specific individuals unto salvation but merely wills that *whosoever* freely accepts the offer be saved. On such a model, if no one should ever accept God's offer, it wouldn't mean God failed any more than ideal human parents must have failed if their kids turn out bad. No, if the hypothetical parents have done everything right on their end, then, setting external factors aside, it must be the kids' fault.

One may counter, however, that even if God's central goals are generic, there may remain crucially important *specific* goals that a generally provident God would lack sufficient control to ensure, for example, that the incarnation occurs at a specific time and place, or that the prophets and apostles produce reliable scriptures. Such goals may be too important for God's central goals to remain dependent on the *chance* – even a highly probable one – that enough creatures, or the right creatures, freely cooperate. Responding to this requires that we reflect further on creaturely freedom and God's resources for risk management.

With respect to creaturely freedom, some suppose that if we have libertarian freedom, then we always have it, such that even if we have every reason in the world to choose A, we could still freely choose not-A instead (Perszyk, 2019: 170).[77] This is a serious misconception. All libertarianism requires is that *choices that ground moral responsibility* be indeterministic and ultimately up to us. Such choices may be few and far between. Indeed, libertarianism is compatible with most of our actions being effectively determined by current circumstances, emotions, habits, desires, and beliefs. As van Inwagen (1989) points out, we often take ourselves to have "conclusive reasons" for our actions, as evidenced by the fact that we don't bother to deliberate about most of what we do. We just "go with the flow" in such a way that doing otherwise isn't even considered an option. For example, when I drive home from work, I take the same route every time unless something, for example, an unanticipated road closure, forces me to reevaluate. Van Inwagen argues that we only have libertarian freedom when we do *not* take ourselves to have conclusive reasons for any single course of action but instead are consciously torn between competing live options. Only under such conditions can we reasonably exercise the control conditions necessary for grounding moral responsibility. In sum, we need only have libertarian freedom *some* of the time, and thus the risk posed to God's specific plans by human freedom is less than risk objectors often suppose.[78]

---

[77] Peckham (2021: 120) seems to think that "consistent" libertarian freedom means *never* being causally determined to act as one does.

[78] Sijuwade (2023) makes a similar point.

Finally, God's ability to manage risk should not be underestimated. In the first place, God has complete, unilateral control over the initial conditions of creation, its causal constraints (i.e., the laws of nature and the causal powers various creatures possess), and his interaction policies with creation (i.e., whether and under what conditions God intervenes in creation, and if so how). Second, as I argued in Section 2.2 on risk management grounds, God does exhaustive contingency planning. For *every* metaphysically possible creaturely scenario, God decides whether to admit it as a causal possibility and what his response shall be should that possibility become actual. Third, given God's power for unilateral intervention, he can preempt creaturely actions when necessary, as in the biblical account of Balaam (Numbers 22:21–38). God can also causally influence people to act in specific ways and preempt undesired contrary inclinations on their part. According to 2 Peter 1:21, this seems to be how God spoke through the prophets. God can also steer evil intentions for his own purposes, as with the judicial hardening of Pharoah (Exodus 9:12; 10:20; 10:27; 11:10), provided God doesn't cause someone to become evil in the first place (James 1:13). Finally, God can use redundancy or backup mechanisms to keep his plans for creation on track. Such mechanisms might include, but are not limited to, sending prophets to call people to repentance and granting post-mortem opportunities for salvation and healing (e.g., purgatory or reincarnation) (Mullins & Sani, 2021).

In sum, I see no reason to think open theism is committed to morally problematic risk-taking on God's part and every reason to think God has the resources to manage whatever risks he takes in a loving, wise, and competent manner, just like an ideal parent.

4.3 It's Not Biblical! The Challenge of Scriptural Prophecy

The next major challenge for open theism is that it fails the test of scriptural fidelity, particularly with respect to prophecy. This objection has no force against open theists who do not follow a religious tradition that regards some text (e.g., the Torah, Bible, or Quran) as divinely inspired scripture. Most open theists, however, do belong to such a tradition. The challenge for them is that their own scriptures sometimes seem to depict God in ways that conflict with open theism. Non-open theists like Ware (2000) and Peckham (2021) leverage those scriptural passages against open theism, whereas open theists like Boyd (2001), Sanders (2007), and Pinnock (2001) argue that such passages are consistent with open theism when properly understood.

Many passages in both Jewish and Christian scriptures, for example, *arguably* suggest either that there is no future contingency (because God has determined everything) or that God has infallible foreknowledge of how future contingencies resolve. Since open theists hold that there is future contingency and deny that God can infallibly foreknow how future contingencies resolve, these passages pose interpretive challenges for Jewish and Christian open theists. In response, I argue that open theists have many ways of accommodating seemingly contrary passages. Because I am not a biblical scholar and because there are many more potentially problematic scriptural passages than I can address, my goal is merely to describe and illustrate the *general strategies* open theists can use to accommodate apparent scriptural counterevidence. Finally, even though I focus on Jewish and Christian scriptures, open theists of other faith traditions can pursue similar strategies with respect to their own scriptures.

There are at least nine such strategies. Thus, for any putatively scriptural text T that is supposedly predictive of event E, open theists may suggest several interpretive possibilities:

(1) T is scriptural and *strongly predictive* of E, such that
    (1a) E is already causally determined but limited in scope and/or specificity.
    (1b) E is something God will ensure, by unilateral action or causal determination if necessary.
(2) T is scriptural and *weakly predictive* of E, such that
    (2a) E is merely probable.
    (2b) E is conditional upon future developments.
        (2b1) E is a conditional natural consequence (conditional form of 1a or 2a).
        (2b2) E is a conditional intended response (conditional form of 1b).
(3) T is scriptural and *nonpredictive* of E, such that
    (3a) T is about E but was written *after the fact*.
    (3b) T is not about E.
        (3b1) T is canonically associated with E via later midrashic readings of T.
        (3b2) T is not even canonically associated with E.
(4) T is *nonscriptural.*

The distinction between strongly and weakly predictive turns on whether T is taken to depict the future as *settled* with respect to E or whether T is taken to depict E merely as a future possibility or probability. To take T as nonpredictive of E is to say that T at most only *appears* to be predictive of E.

I now illustrate how these strategies may be employed to rebut anti–open theism prooftexts. I do *not* claim that my illustrations represent the *only* or *optimal* ways open theists can reasonably construe the passages in question. I only claim that they are plausible responses. Individual open theists may differ about which strategy or combination of strategies yields the most defensible take on any specific passage.

First, on open theism it is no problem for God to know of future events that are already determined (1a) or that God categorically intends to bring about (1b). Deuteronomy 31:20–21 is a plausible example of the former. God predicts that, after the Israelites enter the promised land, "they will turn to other gods and serve them ... and break my covenant." God knows this because he knows "what they are inclined to do even today." That is, knowing the current orientation of his people, God knows inevitably (1a) or, perhaps, with high probability (2a), that many will eventually turn away. Similarly, in Psalm 139 David marvels at God's exhaustive and intimate knowledge of present conditions. Verse 4 says, "before a word is on my tongue, ... you know it altogether." This isn't foreknowing from eternity past everything David ever says, but knowing what he is about to say based on knowledge of David's current thoughts.[79]

As for God's categorical intentions (1b), God's knowledge of "what is to come hereafter" (Isaiah 41:23) ultimately rests on his ability to ensure that what God absolutely wants to happen, happens. Isaiah 46:9–11 says that God declares "the end from the beginning ... saying, 'My counsel shall stand, and I will accomplish all my purpose.'" This is easy for a God who sets the parameters for what's possible in creation and can unilaterally intervene as needed (cf. Section 4.2). We should not assume, however, that everything that ever happens is part of God's categorical purpose or "end" *á la* meticulous providence. When Ephesians 1:11 says God "works all things according to the counsel of his will," this is compatible with a general model of divine providence because, while "all things" is obviously maximal in *scope*, it need not be maximal in *specificity*. If, as open theists believe, God deliberately leaves the future open-ended, then it follows that God's categorical purposes are somewhat *general*.

Second, it is also no problem on open theism for God to know the probable as probable (2a) or the conditional as conditional (2b). Regarding the latter, many biblical prophecies are explicitly conditional (e.g., Jeremiah 26:4–6 and Luke 13:3), whereas others are implicitly conditional. For example, in 1 Samuel 23:9–13 David consults God about what Saul and the men of Keilah "will" do but then thwarts the prophecies by departing from Keilah. The prophecies were thus obviously conditional upon David's remaining in

---

[79] Similarly, some take Psalm 139:16 to mean that every detail of David's future life was foreknown to God. But this reading doesn't fit the embryological context of verses 13–16. Calvin argues that verse 16 is about God's "gradually giving shape and beauty to a confused [embryonic] mass" (Calvin, 1849: 217–218).

Keilah and may plausibly be understood as extrapolations (2b1) from then-current conditions. Similarly, in Isaiah 38:1–5 and Jonah 3:3–10 first Hezekiah and then the Ninevites are told something "will" happen that subsequently does not. Due to Hezekiah's prayer and the Ninevites' repentance, God responds by changing the predicted outcome (2b2), showing that the prophecies were conditional all along. In both Jeremiah 18:7–10 and Ezekiel 33:13–15 it is implied, in fact, that *all* prophecies related to reward and punishment are conditional, even when the condition isn't stated.

Explicitly probabilistic prophecies (2a) are hard to find, but some may be implicitly so. For example, Ezekiel 26:1–21 predicts that the Babylonians will conquer and plunder Tyre, but Ezekiel 29:17–21 later admits that the Babylonians failed to get any significant plunder from Tyre and promises that they will plunder Egypt instead. But this also seems not to have happened (Ulrich, 2000). One way to handle this double case of failed prophecy is to suppose that the predictions reflected what was highly likely to happen at the time and were thus implicitly probabilistic.

Third, many so-called "prophecies" are nonpredictive and thus nonproblematic for open theists. For example, many Hebrew Bible passages said to be "fulfilled" in the life of Jesus are not predictive of him at all, when viewed in their own context (3b1). Matthew 2:15 quotes Hosea 11:1 ("out of Egypt I called my son"), but Hosea is speaking about Israel, not the messiah. Likewise, Matthew 1:23 quotes Isaiah 7:14 ("the virgin shall conceive and bear a son"), but Isaiah is speaking about an event during the reign of Ahaz.[80] Similarly, in John 13:18 Jesus quotes Psalm 41:9 in reference to his coming betrayal, but in context the psalm is about an event in David's life. This type of interpretation, whereby a present event is linked to a past event that it is said to be a "fulfillment" of is known as *midrash* (Pickup, 2008). The connection is one of resemblance or typology, not prediction/fulfillment.

Another possible instance of nonpredictive "prophecy" is that of Daniel 11:2–35, which recounts with high accuracy the defeat of the Persian empire by the Greeks and centuries of subsequent infighting between the Ptolemaic and Seleucid dynasties. The critical consensus is that this passage is an after-the-fact "prophecy" presented as though it were written before the fact (3a). According to Blomberg (2014: 163–165), this is a common feature of apocalyptic writing. He considers it a viable interpretive option for Daniel 11 and other similarly apocalyptic passages.

As for cases (3b2) and (4), I include them for completeness. They have to do with passages that are hermeneutically or textually problematic, for example,

---

[80] The Hebrew word for "virgin" can also mean "young woman."

where the supposition that T is about E or even canonically associated with E derives from a bad interpretation (3b2) or a nonauthentic manuscript tradition (4).

Fourth and finally, in the case of *complex* events like Israel's predicted exodus from Egypt (Exodus 3:19–22) or Jesus's prediction of Peter's denial (Mark 14:27–30), open theists can combine strategies. Regarding the Exodus passage they might say, for example, that certain aspects of that event (e.g., that Pharoah would initially resist) are already determined (1a), that other aspects (e.g., that Pharoah would continue resisting until after the final plague) are ones God will ensure (1b), and that other aspects (e.g., that the Egyptians would send the Israelites off with their riches) are natural consequences conditional upon the plagues (2b1). Regarding Peter's threefold denial before the rooster crows twice, they might say that this is merely an extrapolation from current conditions (1a or 2a) plus God's ability to make a rooster crow on cue (1b or 2b2). Thus, Jesus knew the opposition he was facing and their plans to destroy him (Mark 10:32–34). Jesus also knew that Peter was overconfident (v. 29) and not prepared for the trial he was about to face (vv. 37–38). After Jesus's arrest, Peter's confidence was shaken to the point that he quickly folded under pressure and possibly would have continued denying Christ had not God mercifully poked a rooster twice to reorient Peter's mindset.

In sum, open theists have many interpretive options to meet the challenge of scriptural prophecy. They only need provide *some* defensible combination of (1–4) for any putatively anti–open theistic scriptural passage to deflect the challenge.

4.4 It's Unorthodox! The Challenge of Religious Tradition

The challenge of religious tradition is that open theism is so far out of step with certain religious traditions that adherents of those traditions should not countenance it as a viable theological option. I address this challenge from a Christian context and trust that Jewish and Muslim open theists can adjust for their own contexts.

This challenge obviously assumes that tradition places a *normative* constraint on Christian belief. Some Christian open theists might casually reject that assumption. If the Bible teaches open theism, then who cares what ancient Christians thought? This is a bad response. As a type of testimony, tradition ought to have *some* normative force, for there is a standard epistemic presumption in favor of testimony, and a strong one in favor of expert consensus, when it exists. If we took the opposite presumption and required everyone to establish their trustworthiness *before* listening to them, then no one would ever be able to establish their credentials and we'd never be able to trust anyone about anything. So, unless we have specific reason to think someone untrustworthy, like the boy who repeatedly cried "wolf," we should presume that people are sufficiently honest and competent to deserve the benefit of the doubt when speaking on matters within their purview. If many people with relevant expertise agree on something, this presumption can become quite strong. Thus, if the Church fathers, historically recognized experts on early Christian thought, are generally opposed to central claims of open theism, then Christian open theists need to grapple with that fact. They need reasonable answers to questions like: If open theism is true and supported by scripture, then why *isn't* it better represented in the tradition? Why *shouldn't* the contrary consensus of the tradition (assuming such a consensus exists) hold sway in this case?

Some Christian communities, particularly the Roman Catholic and Eastern Orthodox communities, have a stronger commitment to the normativity of tradition than what a standard testimonial presumption might require. To avoid making my task too easy, I'm going to address the challenge of religious tradition from an Eastern Orthodox (hereafter, "Orthodox") perspective.[81] According to Orthodoxy, the seven ecumenical councils from Nicaea 1 (325 CE) to Nicaea 2 (787 CE) are dogmatically authoritative.[82] Moreover, the general attitude toward Christian tradition is highly conservative. In the famous words of Vincent of Lérins (died c. 445), if a belief or practice in the early Church was held "everywhere, always, and by all," then it remains presumptively binding on Christians today. Conversely, beliefs or practices not well-represented in Church tradition are viewed as innovative and, for that reason, potentially suspect. My goal is to show that open theism remains a permissible theological opinion or *theologoumenon* within an Orthodox context.

Now, in many respects open theism stands in good stead vis-à-vis Christian tradition since it affirms minimal monotheism and is compatible with post-Nicene trinitarian and Christological orthodoxy. Moreover, open theism's commitment to a causally open future finds ample support in early Christian affirmations of creaturely moral freedom after the Fall and a synergistic view of salvation (Karamanolis, 2021: ch. 4). It wasn't until after Augustine's anti-Pelagian crusade, from roughly 410 on, that deterministic ideas started to gain a footing in the Western Church, where Augustine's influence was immense

---

[81] I choose Orthodoxy as my focus because it's both deeply traditional and has no dogmatically binding pronouncements against open theism. Roman Catholicism is trickier because the semi-open theistic views of Peter de Rivo (c. 1420–1490) were condemned by Pope Sixtus IV in 1473 and a similar anti-openness stance was later reaffirmed by the First Vatican Council (Butler, 1930: 254–255).

[82] From the official statements I've seen, the seven ecumenical councils are the one thing all Orthodox clearly accept as binding, so I use that as my criterion for Orthodoxy.

(Boettner, 1932: 365–367). However, the early Church also seems to have widely held that God has specific foreknowledge of human free choices, something open theism denies. Here's a representative quote from John Damascene (c. 676–749): "[The divine nature has the property] of knowing all things ... and seeing into all things clearly by its divine, all-surveying, and immaterial eye, those that belong to the present, the past, and the future before they come to be" (John of Damascus, 2022: 96). Now, a careful contextual reading of that and similar passages from the Church fathers might reveal that some of them can be reconciled with open theism. Though they aren't affirming open theism, perhaps some aren't *exactly* denying it either. After all, open theism doesn't reject divine foreknowledge per se, but only God's foreknowing the outcomes of unresolved future contingencies. One nondismissive way to rebut the challenge of tradition is to show through detailed historical work (if possible) that the Church fathers are far from unified in asserting *the kind of foreknowledge* open theists reject.[83] Since that would take us far outside my expertise, *for the sake of argument* I'm going to *assume* that the Church fathers are *unanimous* in affirming, explicitly or implicitly, that God has EDF. If that is correct, then Christian tradition is in this respect decidedly inconvenient for open theism.

Of course, if the tradition is far less unified on the foreknowledge question than I am assuming it to be – if, for example, open theists can find a few prominent Church fathers who *clearly deny* that God has EDF – then Christian open theists would be in "good company" at least. Even if the view remained a small minority report, the challenge of tradition would lose much of its force. But, alas, it's hard to find *any* clear early affirmations of open theism by someone who *also* had significant authority in the early Church. Calcidius (fourth century) is the clearest example of an early open theist we know of, but he wasn't a Church father.

Given, then, the (assumed) consensus among Church fathers in favor of EDF, it may seem that Christian tradition should exclude open theism. After all, if the Holy Spirit is guiding the Church into "all truth" (John 16:13), and if he apparently didn't guide the Church toward open theism but away from it, then arguably that's because open theism isn't true. Moreover, Jesus promised that "the gates of hell will not prevail" against his Church (Matthew 16:18). If open theists dismiss early Christian tradition on the theory that the Church quickly and collectively drifted into wholesale error due to the malign external influence of Greek philosophy, isn't that calling Jesus a liar? Furthermore, the apostles

---

[83] Gavrilyuk (2004) does this with respect to divine impassibility, arguing that the early Church was not as *absolute* about impassibility as Western medieval theology later held.

repeatedly admonish their successors to preserve "the faith once for all delivered to the saints" (Jude 3), thereby instilling a custodial mindset toward apostolic teaching and practice that the Church fathers regularly reaffirmed. Given Jesus's promise and the strong disposition of the early Church to guard the tradition, suggestions that the early Church went off the rails concerning matters central to the faith should be met with considerable skepticism by Christians. Consequently, if open theists are to face the challenge of tradition head-on, then they need a principled case that those aspects of the tradition pushing against open theism are, at the very least, nonbinding.

In reflecting on the normativity of tradition, Vincent of Lérins' slogan is a good place to start. The three criteria he mentions are *ubiquity* ("everywhere"), *antiquity* ("always"), and *universality* ("by all"). Each is a commonsense guide for evaluating elements of a tradition. All other things equal, views with greater antiquity are likely closer to the origins of a tradition and therefore have better claim to be authentic expressions of it. Likewise, all other things equal, the more universally and ubiquitously a view is held within a community, the better its claim authentically to express that community's tradition. Of course, additional nuance is needed. First, what is the scope of "all" in Vincent's slogan? One can make many strange ideas seem to have strong roots in a tradition by cherry-picking the "right" representatives. Second, ubiquity, antiquity, and universality come in degrees. Taken without qualification, these are *excessively strong* criteria. Since doctrines and practices naturally develop over time, unless we define them somewhat broadly, it may be hard to find *anything* that was literally held everywhere, always, and by all within the early Church. Third, even collectively, these criteria are *not sufficient* for normative status. Suppose the entire early Church believed confidently in a geocentric cosmos. This is not historically implausible (Kuhn, 1957). Would that make geocentrism normative for Christians today? Obviously not. The mere fact that a view *happens* to be popular in a community – perhaps because it was absorbed uncritically from the prevailing zeitgeist – isn't enough to render it normative. Its *centrality* to the beliefs and practices of the community must also be considered. Views concerning Christology, for example, have always been of central importance to Christianity because they bear directly on the Church's understanding of salvation. That's why so much attention in the early Church, including the first six ecumenical councils, was devoted to Christological issues. Geocentrism, on the other hand, despite what some Church leaders thought during the Galileo affair (Finocchiaro, 1989), was tangential to Christianity from the outset and was never an issue in the early Church.

Furthermore, for a view to be present "always" and yet develop over time, it must be present *in an implicit and germinal form* from the get-go. Subsequent developments would then reflect a mostly *internal* process of refinement as the

Church grapples with the apostolic deposit (Scripture plus early oral tradition). For example, the doctrines of the deity of Jesus, the Incarnation, and Trinity are all arguably implicit from the outset, being at least hinted at in the prologue of John's gospel (John 1:1–18). Still, it took centuries for the Church to work out the Trinitarian and Christological implications. The historical development of trinitarian doctrine from the second through fourth centuries, for example, was a complicated process (Dünzl, 2007). Prior to 381, and to some extent afterwards, the Church fathers were not of one mind regarding the Trinity. There were different camps, East and West, using different languages and terminology, and veering sometimes into modalism and sometimes into subordinationism. Nevertheless, after intense debate culminating in the Nicene–Constantinopolitan (381) and Chalcedonian (451) creeds, the orthodox position was hammered out and (mostly) stabilized against the prevailing heresies. In Orthodoxy, ecumenical conciliar pronouncements like the Nicene creed are regarded as dogmatically normative because it is believed that the Holy Spirit worked *through* the debate, discussion, and prayerful reflection on the apostolic deposit to guide the Church toward greater understanding of the central truths of the faith. The contrast between the absence of any serious debate over geocentrism and the intense debates over Christological and Trinitarian issues underscores a fifth criterion, that of *scrutiny*. Some views in Church history were intensely scrutinized over time by large and broadly representative (i.e., ecumenical) groups of Church leaders. Commonsensically, views that survive this kind of vetting process have a much stronger normative claim than views that never receive scrutiny because, like geocentrism, they are mostly just taken for granted.

With this final criterion, I think we have the resources to give an adequate, nondismissive defense of open theism against the challenge of religious tradition within a Christian context:

- Open theism's commitment to a causally and providentially open[84] future has strong support among the Church fathers. From the perspective of Church tradition, open theism's only major suspect commitment is its denial of EDF. But, while no Church fathers clearly deny EDF, it's not entirely clear that all would have affirmed EDF.
- *Even if* all Church fathers would have affirmed EDF, that God has EDF is not a *central* Christian belief. It is more like geocentrism than the deity of Jesus, the Incarnation, and the Trinity. So, as with geocentrism, even the hypothetical presence of a uniform consensus in favor of EDF from the outset should not *ipso facto* place open theism out of bounds.

---

[84] John of Damascus (2022: 155–161), for one, seems clearly to endorse a *general* model of divine providence.

- The noncentrality of EDF is supported by the fact that it was *never collectively scrutinized* by the early Church. The creeds and canons of the seven ecumenical councils say *nothing* about divine foreknowledge. There was never any widespread debate over whether God has EDF, much less one that reached ecumenical proportions. None of open theism's central claims was ever anathematized until long after the East–West schism of 1054 CE, and that only in the Western Church, not in the East.

I submit, then, that while early Church tradition provides little (if any) positive support for open theism's denial of EDF, it doesn't rule it dogmatically out of bounds either. Open theism therefore ought to be considered a permissible theological option not only for big-O Orthodox Christians but a fortiori for less tradition-bound Christians who aren't otherwise confessionally committed to EDF.

5 Conclusion

With that, I draw this Element to a close. If my explication of, case for, and defense of open theism have been reasonably accurate, then open theism deserves serious consideration from all minimal monotheists. Given more space, I would love to have explored the implications of open theism for religious practice. As matters stand, I can only suggest that readers interested in that topic start with Pinnock et al. (1994: ch. 5) and Sanders (2007: ch. 8).

References

Anderson, J. N. (2019). "May it have happened, Lord!": Open theism and past-directed prayers. In B. H. Arbour, ed., *Philosophical Essays against Open Theism*. New York: Routledge, pp. 121–139.

Basinger, D. (1988). *Divine Power in Process Theism: A Philosophical Critique*. Albany, NY: SUNY Press.

Basinger, D. (1996). *The Case for Freewill Theism: A Philosophical Assessment*. Downers Grove, IL: InterVarsity Press.

Boettner, L. (1932). *The Reformed Doctrine of Predestination*. Grand Rapids, MI: Eerdmans.

Boyd, G. A. (1997). *God at War: The Bible and Spiritual Conflict*. Downers Grove, IL: InterVarsity Press.

Boyd, G. A. (2001). *God of the Possible: A Biblical Introduction to the Open View of God*. Grand Rapids, MI: Baker.

Boyd, G. A. (2003). Neo-Molinism and the infinite intelligence of God. *Philosophia Christi* 5, 187–204.

Boyd, G. A. (2010). Two ancient (and modern) motivations for ascribing exhaustively definite foreknowledge to God: A historic overview and critical assessment. *Religious Studies* 46(1), 41–59.

Butler, Cuthbert. (1930). *The Vatican Council*, vol. 2. London: Longmans, Green and Co.

Calvin, J. (1849). *Commentary on the Book of Psalms*, vol. 5, trans. J. Anderson. Edinburgh: Calvin Translation Society.

Cobb, J. B., Jr. , & Griffin, D. R. (1976). *Process Theology: An Introductory Exposition*. Louisville, KY: Westminster John Knox Press.

Cobb, J. B., Jr., & Pinnock, C. H., eds. (2000). *Searching for an Adequate God: A Dialogue between Process and Free Will Theists*. Grand Rapids, MI: Eerdmans.

Craig, W. L. (1990). *Divine Foreknowledge and Human Freedom*. Leiden: Brill.

Craig, W. L. & Smith, Q. (2008). *Einstein, Relativity, and Absolute Simultaneity*. London: Routledge.

Creel, R. E. (1986). *Divine Impassibility: An Essay in Philosophical Theology*. Cambridge: Cambridge University Press.

Crisp, T. (2007). Presentism and the grounding objection. *Noûs* 41(1), 90–109.

Den Boeft, J. (1970). *Calcidius on Fate: His Doctrines and Sources*. Leiden: Brill.

Dolezal, J. (2011). *God without Parts: Divine Simplicity and the Metaphysics of God's Absoluteness*. Eugene, OR: Pickwick.

Dünzl, F. (2007). *A Brief History of the Doctrine of the Trinity in the Early Church*. New York: T&T Clark.

Edwards, J. (2009 [1754]). *Freedom of the Will*. Vancouver: Eremitical Press.

Effler, R. R. (1962). *John Duns Scotus and the Principle "Omne quod movetur ab alio movetur."* St. Bonaventure, NY: Franciscan Institute.

Feinberg, J. S. (2001). *No One Like Him: The Doctrine of God*. Wheaton, IL: Crossway.

Finch, A. & Rea, M. (2008). Presentism and Ockham's way out. *Oxford Studies in Philosophy of Religion* 1, 1–17.

Finocchiaro, M. A. (1989). *The Galileo Affair: A Documentary History*. Berkeley, CA: University of California Press.

Fischer, J. M. (2016). *Our Fate: Essays on God and Free Will*. Oxford: Oxford University Press.

Flint, T. P. (1990). Hasker's "God, time, and knowledge." *Philosophical Studies* 60(1–2), 103–115.

Flint, T. P. (1998). *Divine Providence: The Molinist Account*. Ithaca, NY: Cornell University Press.

Fretheim, T. E. (1984). *The Suffering of God: An Old Testament Perspective*. Philadelphia: Fortress.

Gavrilyuk, P. (2004). *The Suffering of the Impassible God: The Dialectics of Patristic Thought*. Oxford: Oxford University Press.

Gersh, S. (1986). *Middle Platonism and Neoplatonism: The Latin Tradition*. Notre Dame, IN: University of Notre Dame Press.

Grössl, J. & Vicens, L. (2014). Closing the door on limited-risk open theism. *Faith and Philosophy* 31(4), 475–485.

Hansson, S. O. (2013). *The Ethics of Risk: Ethical Analysis in an Uncertain World*. New York: Palgrave Macmillan.

Hart, M. J. & Hill, D. J. (2022). *Does God Intend that Sin Occur?* London: Palgrave Macmillan.

Hasker, W. (1989). *God, Time, and Knowledge*. Ithaca, NY: Cornell University Press.

Hasker, W. (2004). *Providence, Evil and the Openness of God*. London: Routledge.

Hasker, W. (2021). Future truth and freedom. *International Journal for Philosophy of Religion* 90(2), 109–119.

Hess, E. (2015). Arguing from Molinism to neo-Molinism. *Philosophia Christi* 17(2), 331–351.

Hume, D. (1990 [1779]). *Dialogues Concerning Natural Religion*. London: Penguin.

Hunt, D. P. (1999). On Augustine's way out. *Faith and Philosophy* 16(1), 3–26.

Hunt, D. P. (2001). The simple foreknowledge view. In J. K. Beilby & P. R. Eddy, eds., *Divine Foreknowledge: Four Views*. Downers Grove, IL: InterVarsity Press, pp. 65–114.

Hunt, D. P. (2009a). Contra Hasker: Why simple foreknowledge is still useful. *Journal of the Evangelical Theological Society* 52(3): 545–550.

Hunt, D. P. (2009b). What does God know? The problems of open theism. In P. Copan & W. L. Craig, eds., *Contending with Christianity's Critics*. Nashville, TN: B&H, pp. 265–282.

John of Damascus. (2022). *On the Orthodox Faith*, trans. N. Russell. Yonkers, NY: St. Vladimir's Seminary Press.

Jorgenson, J. (1992). Predestination according to divine foreknowledge in patristic tradition. In J. Meyendorff & R. Tobias, eds. *Salvation in Christ: A Lutheran–Orthodox Dialogue*. Minneapolis, MN: Augsburg Fortress, pp. 159–169, 182–183.

Kane, R. (2005). *A Contemporary Introduction to Free Will*. Oxford: Oxford University Press.

Karamanolis, G. (2021). *The Philosophy of Early Christianity*, 2nd ed. London: Routledge.

Klein, W. W. (2015). *The New Chosen People: A Corporate View of Election*, rev. ed. Eugene, OR: Wipf & Stock.

Kuhn, T. (1957). *The Copernican Revolution: Planetary Astronomy in the Development of Western Thought*. Cambridge, MA: Harvard University Press.

Kvanvig, J. L. (2011). *Destiny and Deliberation: Essays in Philosophical Theology*. Oxford: Oxford University Press.

Leithart, P. J. (2004). Evangelicals in the dock. *First Things* 141(March), 9–11.

Lewis, D. (1973). *Counterfactuals*. Oxford: Blackwell.

Lewis, D. (1986a). *On the Plurality of Worlds*. Oxford: Blackwell.

Lewis, D. (1986b). A subjectivist's guide to objective chance. In D. Lewis, *Philosophical Papers*, vol. 2, pp. 83–132. Oxford: Oxford University Press.

Lodahl, M. (2009). The (brief) openness debate in Islamic theology. In T. J. Oord, ed., *Creation Made Free: Open Theology Engaging Science*. Eugene, OR: Pickwick, pp. 53–68.

Lossky, V. (1978). *Orthodox Theology: An Introduction*. Crestwood, NY: St. Vladimir's Seminary Press.

Mawson, T. J. (2019). *The Divine Attributes*. Cambridge: Cambridge University Press.

McCall, S. (1994). *A Model of the Universe: Space-Time, Probability, and Decision*. Oxford: Clarendon Press.

McCann, H. (2005). The author of sin? *Faith and Philosophy* 22(2), 144–159.

Mullins, R. T. (2016). *The End of the Timeless God*. Oxford: Oxford University Press.

Mullins, R. T. (2020). *God and Emotion.* Cambridge: Cambridge University Press.

Mullins, R. T. (2022). From divine timemaker to divine watchmaker. In M. Schmücker *et al.*, eds., *Temporality and Eternity: Nine Perspectives on God and Time.* Boston: De Gruyter, pp. 33–56.

Mullins, R. T. & Sani, E. (2021). Open theism and risk management: A philosophical and biological perspective. *Zygon* 56(3), 591–613.

Nagasawa, Y. (2017). *Maximal God: A New Defence of Perfect Being Theology.* Oxford: Oxford University Press.

Ockham, W. (1983). *Predestination, God's Foreknowledge, and Future Contingents*, 2nd ed. Indianapolis: Hackett.

O'Keefe, T. (2005). *Epicurus on Freedom.* Cambridge: Cambridge University Press.

Peckham, J. C. (2021). *Divine Attributes: Knowing the Covenantal God of Scripture.* Grand Rapids, MI: Baker.

Pereboom, D. (2011). Theological determinism and divine providence. In K. Perszyk, ed., *Molinism: The Contemporary Debate.* Oxford: Oxford University Press, pp. 262–280.

Perszyk, K. (2019). Open theism and the soteriological problem of evil. In B. H. Arbour, ed., *Philosophical Essays against Open Theism.* New York: Routledge, pp. 159–177.

Pickup, M. (2008). New Testament interpretation of the Old Testament: The theological rationale of midrashic exegesis. *Journal of the Evangelical Theological Society* 51(2), 353–381.

Pike, N. (1965). Divine omniscience and voluntary action. *The Philosophical Review* 74(1), 27–46.

Pinnock, C., Rice, R., Sanders, J., Hasker, W., & Basinger, D. (1994). *The Openness of God: A Biblical Challenge to the Traditional Understanding of God.* Downers Grove, IL: InterVarsity Press.

Pinnock, C. H. (2001). *Most Moved Mover: A Theology of God's Openness.* Grand Rapids, MI: Baker.

Plantinga, A. (1974). *The Nature of Necessity.* Oxford: Clarendon Press.

Plantinga, A. (1986). On Ockham's way out. *Faith and Philosophy* 3(3), 235–269.

Prior, A. N. (2003). *Papers on Time and Tense*, 2nd ed. Oxford: Clarendon Press.

Ramsay, A. (1748). *The Philosophical Principles of Natural and Revealed Religion.* Glasgow: Robert Foulis.

Rhoda, A. R. (2008). Generic open theism and some varieties thereof. *Religious Studies* 44(2), 225–234.

Rhoda, A. R. (2009). Beyond the chessmaster analogy: Game theory and divine providence. In T. J. Oord, ed., *Creation Made Free: Open Theology Engaging Science*. Eugene, OR: Pickwick, pp. 151–175.

Rhoda, A. R. (2010). Gratuitous evil and divine providence. *Religious Studies* 46, 281–302.

Rhoda, A. R. (2014). Foreknowledge and fatalism: Why divine timelessness doesn't help. In L. N. Oaklander, ed., *Debates in the Metaphysics of Time*. London: Continuum, pp. 253–274.

Rhoda, A. R. (2017). Bootstrapping divine foreknowledge? Comments on Fischer. *Science, Religion & Culture* 4(2), 72–78.

Rhoda, A. R. (2022). Divine providence and the problem of evil. *Encounter* 82(2), 1–37.

Rhoda, A. R., Boyd, G. A., & Belt, T. G. (2006). Open theism, omniscience, and the nature of the future. *Faith and Philosophy* 23(4), 432–459.

Rice, R. (1985). *God's Foreknowledge & Man's Free Will*. Eugene, OR: Wipf & Stock.

Rissler, J. (2006). Open theism: Does God risk or hope? *Religious Studies* 42(1), 63–74.

Robinson, M. D. (2003). *The Storms of Providence: Navigating the Waters of Calvinism, Arminianism, and Open Theism*. Lanham, MD: University Press of America.

Rogers, K. (2008). *Anselm on Freedom*. Oxford: Oxford University Press.

Rudavsky, T. M. (2000). *Time Matters: Time, Creation, and Cosmology in Medieval Jewish Philosophy*. Albany, NY: SUNY Press.

Sanders, J. (1997). Why simple foreknowledge offers no more providential control than the openness of God. *Faith and Philosophy* 14(1), 26–40.

Sanders, J. (1998). *The God Who Risks: A Theology of Providence*. Downers Grove, IL: InterVarsity Press.

Sanders, J. (2007). *The God Who Risks: A Theology of Divine Providence*, 2nd ed. Downers Grove, IL: InterVarsity Press.

Schabel, C. (2000). *Theology at Paris, 1316–1345: Peter Auriol and the Problem of Divine Foreknowledge and Future Contingents*. Aldershot, UK: Ashgate.

Schmid, J. C. (2022). From modal collapse to providential collapse. *Philosophia* 50(3), 1413–1435.

Schmid, J. C. & Linford, D. J. (2023). *Existential Inertia and Classical Theistic Proofs*. Springer.

Schmid, M. (2021). *God in Motion: A Critical Exploration of the Open Theism Debate*. Waco, TX: Baylor University Press.

Seymour, A. E. (2015). *Presentism, Propositions, and Persons: A Systematic Case for All-Falsism*, diss. University of Notre Dame.

Sharples, R. W. (1983). *Alexander of Aphrodisias on Fate: Text, Translation, and Commentary*. London: Duckworth.

Sijuwade, J. R. (2023). Elucidating open theism. *International Journal for Philosophy of Religion*. 94(2), 151–175.

Stewart, R. B. (2019). On open theism either God has false beliefs, or I can know something that God cannot. In B. H. Arbour, ed., *Philosophical Essays against Open Theism*. New York: Routledge, pp. 110–118.

Swenson, P. (2016). Ability, foreknowledge, and explanatory dependence. *Australasian Journal of Philosophy* 94(4), 658–671.

Swinburne, R. (2016). *The Coherence of Theism*, 2nd ed. Oxford: Oxford University Press.

Taylor, R. (1992). *Metaphysics*, 4th ed. Englewood Cliffs, NJ: Prentice Hall.

Todd, P. (2014). Against limited foreknowledge. *Philosophia* 42(2), 523–538.

Todd, P. (2021). *The Open Future: Why Future Contingents Are All False*. Oxford: Oxford University Press.

Todd, P. (2023). Foreknowledge requires determinism. *Philosophy and Phenomenological Research* 107(1), 125–146.

Tuggy, D. (2007). Three roads to open theism. *Faith and Philosophy* 24(1), 28–51.

Ulrich, D. (2000). Dissonant prophecy in Ezekiel 26 and 29. *Bulletin for Biblical Research* 10(1), 121–141.

van Inwagen, P. (1989). When is the will free? *Philosophical Perspectives* 3, 399–422.

van Inwagen, P. (2008). What does an omniscient being know about the future? *Oxford Studies in Philosophy of Religion* 1, 216–230.

Ware, B. A. (2000). *God's Lesser Glory: The Diminished God of Open Theism*. Wheaton, IL: Crossway.

Wasserman, R. (2021). Freedom, foreknowledge, and dependence. *Noûs* 55(3), 603–622.

White, H. (2016). Theological determinism and the "authoring sin" objection. In D. E. Alexander & D. M. Johnson, eds., *Calvinism and the Problem of Evil*. Eugene, OR: Pickwick, pp. 78–95.

Willard, D. (1998). *The Divine Conspiracy*. New York: HarperCollins.

Wolterstorff, N. (1991). Divine simplicity. *Philosophical Perspectives* 5, 531–552.

Wright, R. K. M. (1996). *No Place for Sovereignty: What's Wrong with Freewill Theism*. Downers Grove, IL: InterVarsity Press.

To my wife Heather. Your loving support has made all the difference.

Cambridge Elements ⁼

Religion and Monotheism

Paul K. Moser

Loyola University Chicago

Paul K. Moser is Professor of Philosophy at Loyola University Chicago. He is the author of God in Moral Experience; *Paul's Gospel of Divine Self-Sacrifice; The Divine Goodness of Jesus; Divine Guidance; Understanding Religious Experience; The God Relationship; The Elusive God* (winner of national book award from the Jesuit Honor Society); *The Evidence for God; The Severity of God; Knowledge and Evidence* (all Cambridge University Press); and *Philosophy after Objectivity* (Oxford University Press); co-author of *Theory of Knowledge* (Oxford University Press); editor of *Jesus and Philosophy* (Cambridge University Press) and *The Oxford Handbook of Epistemology* (Oxford University Press); co-editor of *The Wisdom of the Christian Faith* (Cambridge University Press). He is the co-editor with Chad Meister of the book series *Cambridge Studies in Religion, Philosophy, and Society.*

Chad Meister

Affiliate Scholar, Ansari Institute for Global Engagement with Religion, University of Notre Dame

Chad Meister is Affiliate Scholar at the Ansari Institute for Global Engagement with Religion at the University of Notre Dame. His authored and co-authored books include *Evil: A Guide for the Perplexed* (Bloomsbury Academic, 2nd edition); *Introducing Philosophy of Religion* (Routledge); *Introducing Christian Thought* (Routledge, 2nd edition); and *Contemporary Philosophical Theology* (Routledge). He has edited or co-edited the following: *The Oxford Handbook of Religious Diversity* (Oxford University Press); *Debating Christian Theism* (Oxford University Press); with Paul Moser, *The Cambridge Companion to the Problem of Evil* (Cambridge University Press); and with Charles Taliaferro, *The History of Evil* (Routledge, in six volumes). He is the co-editor with Paul Moser of the book series *Cambridge Studies in Religion, Philosophy, and Society.*

About the Series

This Cambridge Element series publishes original concise volumes on monotheism and its significance. Monotheism has occupied inquirers since the time of the Biblical patriarch, and it continues to attract interdisciplinary academic work today. Engaging, current, and concise, the Elements benefit teachers, researched, and advanced students in religious studies, Biblical studies, theology, philosophy of religion, and related fields.

Cambridge Elements ≡

Religion and Monotheism

Elements in the Series

Monotheism, Suffering, and Evil
Michael L. Peterson

Necessary Existence and Monotheism: An Avicennian Account of the Islamic Conception of Divine Unity
Mohammad Saleh Zarepour

Islam and Monotheism
Celene Ibrahim

Freud's Monotheism
William Parsons

Monotheism in Christian Liturgy
Joris Geldhof

Monotheism and the Suffering of Animals in Nature
Christopher Southgate

Monotheism and Social Justice
Robert Karl Gnuse

Monotheism and Narrative Development of the Divine Character in the Hebrew Bible
Mark McEntire

God and Being
Nathan Lyons

Monotheism and Divine Aggression
Collin Cornell

Jewish Monotheism and Slavery
Catherine Hezser

Open Theism
Alan R. Rhoda

A full series listing is available at: www.cambridge.org/er&m

Printed in the United States
by Baker & Taylor Publisher Services